*Always Remember Who You Are*

# THE AZRIELI SERIES OF HOLOCAUST SURVIVOR MEMOIRS: PUBLISHED TITLES

## ENGLISH TITLES

Judy Abrams, *Tenuous Threads*/ Eva Felsenburg Marx, *One of the Lucky Ones*

Amek Adler, *Six Lost Years*

Molly Applebaum, *Buried Words*

Claire Baum, *The Hidden Package*

Bronia and Joseph Beker, *Joy Runs Deeper*

Tibor Benyovits, *Unsung Heroes*

Max Bornstein, *If Home Is Not Here*

Felicia Carmelly, *Across the Rivers of Memory*

Tommy Dick, *Getting Out Alive*

Marian Domanski, *Fleeing from the Hunter*

John Freund, *Spring's End*

Myrna Goldenberg (Editor), *Before All Memory Is Lost: Women's Voices from the Holocaust*

René Goldman, *A Childhood Adrift*

Elly Gotz, *Flights of Spirit*

Ibolya Grossman and Andy Réti, *Stronger Together*

Pinchas Gutter, *Memories in Focus*

Anna Molnár Hegedűs, *As the Lilacs Bloomed*

Rabbi Pinchas Hirschprung, *The Vale of Tears*

Bronia Jablon, *A Part of Me*

Helena Jockel, *We Sang in Hushed Voices*

Eddie Klein, *Inside the Walls*

Michael Kutz, *If, By Miracle*

Nate Leipciger, *The Weight of Freedom*

Alex Levin, *Under the Yellow and Red Stars*

Fred Mann, *A Drastic Turn of Destiny*

Michael Mason, *A Name Unbroken*

Leslie Meisels with Eva Meisels, *Suddenly the Shadow Fell*

Leslie Mezei, *A Tapestry of Survival*

Muguette Myers, *Where Courage Lives*

David Newman, *Hope's Reprise*

Arthur Ney, *W Hour*

Felix Opatowski, *Gatehouse to Hell*

Marguerite Élias Quddus, *In Hiding*

Maya Rakitova, *Behind the Red Curtain*

Henia Reinhartz, *Bits and Pieces*

Betty Rich, *Little Girl Lost*

Paul-Henri Rips, *E/96: Fate Undecided*

Margrit Rosenberg Stenge, *Silent Refuge*

Steve Rotschild, *Traces of What Was*

Judith Rubinstein, *Dignity Endures*

Martha Salcudean, *In Search of Light*

Kitty Salsberg and Ellen Foster, *Never Far Apart*

Joseph Schwarzberg, *Dangerous Measures*

Zuzana Sermer, *Survival Kit*

Rachel Shtibel, *The Violin*/ Adam Shtibel, *A Child's Testimony*

Maxwell Smart, *Chaos to Canvas*

Gerta Solan, *My Heart Is At Ease*

Zsuzsanna Fischer Spiro, *In Fragile Moments*/ Eva Shainblum, *The Last Time*

George Stern, *Vanished Boyhood*

Willie Sterner, *The Shadows Behind Me*

Ann Szedlecki, *Album of My Life*

William Tannenzapf, *Memories from the Abyss*/ Renate Krakauer, *But I Had a Happy Childhood*

Elsa Thon, *If Only It Were Fiction*

Agnes Tomasov, *From Generation to Generation*

Joseph Tomasov, *From Loss to Liberation*

Sam Weisberg, *Carry the Torch*/ Johnny Jablon, *A Lasting Legacy*

Leslie Vertes, *Alone in the Storm*

Anka Voticky, *Knocking on Every Door*

TITRES FRANÇAIS

Judy Abrams, *Retenue par un fil*/ Eva Felsen-
   burg Marx, *Une question de chance*
Claire Baum, *Le Colis caché*
Bronia et Joseph Beker, *Plus forts que le*
   *malheur*
Max Bornstein, *Citoyen de nulle part*
Tommy Dick, *Objectif: survivre*
Marian Domanski, *Traqué*
John Freund, *La Fin du printemps*
René Goldman, *Une enfance à la dérive*
Anna Molnár Hegedűs, *Pendant la saison*
   *des lilas*
Helena Jockel, *Nous chantions en sourdine*
Michael Kutz, *Si, par miracle*
Nate Leipciger, *Le Poids de la liberté*
Alex Levin, *Étoile jaune, étoile rouge*
Fred Mann, *Un terrible revers de fortune*
Michael Mason, *Au fil d'un nom*
Leslie Meisels, *Soudains, les ténèbres*
Muguette Myers, *Les Lieux du courage*
Arthur Ney, *L'Heure W*

Felix Opatowski, *L'Antichambre de l'enfer*
Marguerite Élias Quddus, *Cachée*
Henia Reinhartz, *Fragments de ma vie*
Betty Rich, *Seule au monde*
Paul-Henri Rips, *Matricule E/96*
Steve Rotschild, *Sur les traces du passé*
Kitty Salsberg et Ellen Foster, *Unies dans*
   *l'épreuve*
Zuzana Sermer, *Trousse de survie*
Rachel Shtibel, *Le Violon*/ Adam Shtibel,
   *Témoignage d'un enfant*
George Stern, *Une jeunesse perdue*
Willie Sterner, *Les Ombres du passé*
Ann Szedlecki, *L'Album de ma vie*
William Tannenzapf, *Souvenirs de l'abîme*/
   Renate Krakauer, *Le Bonheur de l'innocence*
Elsa Thon, *Que renaisse demain*
Agnes Tomasov, *De génération en génération*
Leslie Vertes, *Seul dans la tourmente*
Anka Voticky, *Frapper à toutes les portes*

# Always Remember Who You Are

*Anita Helfgott Ekstein*

THE AZRIELI FOUNDATION
www.azrielifoundation.org

Cover and book design by Mark Goldstein
Endpaper maps by Martin Gilbert
Map on page xxv by François Blanc

LIBRARY AND ARCHIVES CANADA CATALOGUING IN PUBLICATION

Ekstein, Anita Helfgott, 1934– author. Always Remember Who You Are/ Anita Helfgott Ekstein

(Azrieli series of Holocaust survivor memoirs. Series xi)
Includes bibliographical references and index. Canadiana 20190151080
ISBN 978-1-988065-53-3 (softcover) · 8 7 6 5 4 3 2 1

1. Ekstein, Anita Helfgott, 1934– — Childhood and youth. 2. Holocaust, Jewish (1939–1945) — Personal narratives. 3. Holocaust survivors — Poland — Biography. 4. Jews — Poland — Biography. 5. Holocaust, Jewish (1939–1945) — Poland — Biography. 6. Orphans — Canada — Biography. 7. Autobiographies. I. Azrieli Foundation, issuing body. II. Ekstein, Anita Helfgott, 1934–. Alway Remember Who You Are. III. Series: Azrieli series of Holocaust survivor memoirs. Series xi.

LCC DS134.72.E47 A3 2019      DDC 940.53/18092 — DC23

PRINTED IN CANADA

# The Azrieli Series of Holocaust Survivor Memoirs

Naomi Azrieli, Publisher

Jody Spiegel, Program Director
Arielle Berger, Managing Editor
Matt Carrington, Editor
Devora Levin, Assistant Editor
Elizabeth Lasserre, Senior Editor, French-Language Editions
Elin Beaumont, Community and Education Initiatives
Catherine Person, Education and Academic Initiatives/French Editor
Stephanie Corazza, Academic and Education Initiatives
Marc-Olivier Cloutier, School and Education Initiatives
Elizabeth Banks, Digital Asset Curator and Archivist
Catherine Quintal, Digital Communications Assistant

Mark Goldstein, Art Director
François Blanc, Cartographer
Bruno Paradis, Layout, French-Language Editions

# Contents

Series Preface                                          xi

About the Glossary                                      xiii

Introduction *by Beth A. Griech-Polelle*               xv

Map                                                     xxv

Family Tree                                             xxvi–xxvii

Foreword *by Ruth Ekstein*                             xxxi


Cherished                                               1

The Horrors Begin                                       9

Miraculous Escapes                                      19

A Lonely Existence                                      29

Into the Unknown                                        41

Afraid to Be Jewish                                     49

No Longer a Refugee                                     67

The Love of My Life                                     81

The Challenges and Joys of Motherhood                  93

Returning to My Roots                                   111

Branching Out                                           123

Epilogue                                                135


Glossary                                                143

Photographs                                             159

Index                                                   179

# Series Preface: In their own words...

*In telling these stories, the writers have liberated themselves. For so many years we did not speak about it, even when we became free people living in a free society. Now, when at last we are writing about what happened to us in this dark period of history, knowing that our stories will be read and live on, it is possible for us to feel truly free. These unique historical documents put a face on what was lost, and allow readers to grasp the enormity of what happened to six million Jews — one story at a time.*

> David J. Azrieli, C.M., C.Q., M.Arch
> Holocaust survivor and founder, The Azrieli Foundation

Since the end of World War II, approximately 40,000 Jewish Holocaust survivors have immigrated to Canada. Who they are, where they came from, what they experienced and how they built new lives for themselves and their families are important parts of our Canadian heritage. The Azrieli Foundation's Holocaust Survivor Memoirs Program was established in 2005 to preserve and share the memoirs written by those who survived the twentieth-century Nazi genocide of the Jews of Europe and later made their way to Canada. The program is guided by the conviction that each survivor of the Holocaust has a remarkable story to tell, and that such stories play an important role in education about tolerance and diversity.

Millions of individual stories are lost to us forever. By preserving the stories written by survivors and making them widely available to a broad audience, the Azrieli Foundation's Holocaust Survivor Memoirs Program seeks to sustain the memory of all those who perished at the hands of hatred, abetted by indifference and apathy. The personal accounts of those who survived against all odds are as different as the people who wrote them, but all demonstrate the courage, strength, wit and luck that it took to prevail and survive in such terrible adversity. The memoirs are also moving tributes to people — strangers and friends — who risked their lives to help others, and who, through acts of kindness and decency in the darkest of moments, frequently helped the persecuted maintain faith in humanity and courage to endure. These accounts offer inspiration to all, as does the survivors' desire to share their experiences so that new generations can learn from them.

The Holocaust Survivor Memoirs Program collects, archives and publishes select survivor memoirs and makes the print editions available free of charge to educational institutions and Holocaust-education programs across Canada. They are also available for sale online to the general public. All revenues to the Azrieli Foundation from the sales of the Azrieli Series of Holocaust Survivor Memoirs go toward the publishing and educational work of the memoirs program.

~

The Azrieli Foundation would like to express appreciation to the following people for their invaluable efforts in producing this book: Omer Bartov, Doris Bergen, Mark Duffus (Maracle Inc.), Ashley Rayner, Susan Roitman, Dr. Grzegorz Rossoliński-Lieb, Mia Spiro, and Margie Wolfe and Emma Rodgers of Second Story Press. A special thank-you to Adara Goldberg, who dedicated many hours of her time to researching and editing the first draft of Anita Ekstein's memoir.

# About the Glossary

The following memoir contains a number of terms, concepts and historical references that may be unfamiliar to the reader. For information on major organizations; significant historical events and people; geographical locations; religious and cultural terms; and foreign-language words and expressions that will help give context and background to the events described in the text, please see the glossary beginning on page 143.

# Introduction

On August 23, 1939, Adolf Hitler and Joseph Stalin agreed to a historic non-aggression pact that shocked the world. How could ideological enemies, such as the Nazis and the Communists, agree to not attack one another in the event of a war? Although most onlookers could not know this, there were secret protocols attached to the non-aggression pact, in which Hitler invited Stalin to take portions of Poland and other parts of Eastern Europe under Soviet control. In return, Hitler believed that he had eliminated one of the causes of Germany's defeat in World War I: Germany having to fight on two fronts simultaneously. What might a pact from the summer of 1939 have to do with a five-year-old Jewish girl living in Poland?

Anita Helfgott Ekstein's memoir lands the reader right in the region where Hitler and Stalin partitioned Poland, with Stalin's forces taking the part of eastern Poland where young Anita and her parents were living. Anita's story underscores, at least from the perspective of a child, what it was like to live in an ethnically and religiously diverse region of Jews, Poles and Ukrainians, and then Russians and Germans. This is an area of the world that historian Timothy Snyder has termed the "Bloodlands." This highly charged, volatile region would experience Soviet occupation and, as the Soviet forces retreated in 1941 when Germany violated the non-aggression pact, Ukrainian acts of violence against the local population and then German domination.

However, the mixture of identities in the area, which contributed to the danger and turbulence at that time, would ultimately be a reason for Anita's survival, as would her ability to speak fluent Polish.

For a young child, experiencing the outbreak of war on September 1, 1939, then the division of Poland and its occupation under the Soviets, meant turmoil and shortages, particularly of food. For those Jews living in Soviet-occupied Poland from 1939–1941, there was also a general lack of knowledge about what the Nazis were doing to Jews under German occupation. Due to severe censorship, even members of Anita's family living in German-occupied areas could not adequately communicate the details of their experiences. This ignorance about the fate of Jews living under Nazi oppression influenced Anita's parents' ability to make good decisions. And so, when on June 22, 1941, over three million German soldiers and their satellite troops invaded Soviet-occupied territory, Anita's parents decided not to follow the retreating Soviet army further eastwards into the unknown.

As the Soviet forces left eastern Poland, many local Ukrainians rose up against their neighbours in violent pogroms. Accusing local Poles and Jews of being in league with the Soviets, they saw this temporary lack of rule as an opportunity to overthrow their supposed oppressors. For Anita and her parents, hiding in a barn spared them from the days of violence directed at the Jewish population. During these persecutions, Jews often had to rely on the goodness of gentile neighbours who were willing to risk punishment for aiding Jews. Once the looting and killings quieted down, Jews were sometimes able to return to their own apartments. However, the awareness of their precarious position was now ever-present, and even young children could feel the fear of an unknown future.

For the Jews of this region, life as they had known it was about to be irrevocably changed. Hitler was after *Lebensraum* (living space) for the "Aryan" people, but with each successful conquest of new territory, he added to his "Jewish problem" as the bulk of the European Jewish population was centred in Poland and in Soviet-occupied territory. As the Nazi war machine advanced further inside Soviet territory, the events of the November 1938 Kristallnacht pogrom in Germany were repeated: Jewish stores and homes were attacked, Jewish houses of worship were destroyed or desecrated, Jews were beaten and murdered. All of this took place in front of the gentile population, demonstrating to the locals the proper way to interact with Jews. Unlike in Germany, however, the German military that entered Soviet territory was accompanied by execution squads known as the Einsatzgruppen. Made up of units of SS and police, the Einsatzgruppen unleashed terror on the Jewish population, massacring over a million Jews and tens of thousands of others deemed undesirable by the Nazis in open pits.

As the Germans took over regions, they introduced antisemitic legislation that was transplanted from the heart of Nazi Germany and aimed to destroy Jews both economically and socially. Curfews, limited shopping hours, restrictions on rations, loss of employment, segregation from the gentile population and curtailing of education were only some of the ways in which the Nazis sought to bring about the social death of the Jewish community. By limiting interactions between Jews and gentiles, and by enforcing Nazi racial stereotypes, Jews were becoming increasingly isolated from the larger European community to which they had once belonged, and the general population was becoming increasingly indifferent to the fate of the Jews.

Once the Nazis claimed dominion over eastern Poland, Jews living in the area where Anita grew up were absorbed into the Nazi-occupied area of Poland called the *Generalgouvernement*, General Government. This region, envisioned as a dumping ground for those the Nazis considered undesirable, figured into Nazi schemes to reshape the demographics of Eastern Europe. In the parts of western Poland that had been incorporated into Greater Germany, ethnic Germans from the east were resettled in areas that were cleared of Poles and Jews, who were transferred eastward to make room for the "Aryan" population. Jews already living in eastern Poland found themselves suddenly facing numerous rules and restrictions imposed by the Nazis in order to subjugate and isolate them. For children like Anita, this was the end of a true childhood free from cares and worries.

By October 1941, Anita's family had been rounded up and placed in the Skole ghetto. Although this ghetto did not have barbed wire or a fence around it, everyone had to comply with the regulations regarding curfew, and only those who had been selected for work outside the ghetto could leave the Jewish section of Skole. Inside the ghetto, complete strangers were forced to live together in extremely overcrowded and unhygienic apartments. To receive rations, all adults needed a work identity card, but the quantity of food allocated to the ghettos by the Nazis kept most adults at starvation level. Smuggling became a daily necessity to maintain the health of at least some of the ghetto inhabitants. Younger adults were taken out of the ghetto to perform physically demanding labour such as clearing bombed-out roads and repairing damaged train tracks and destroyed buildings, while older adults were generally left behind in the ghetto to care for the children. Throughout this period, there were frequent *Aktionen*, roundups, inside the ghetto, and those who were caught were taken away to be killed. The recollections of young children like Anita tell of how strangers kept coming and going from their overcrowded apartments, adding to their feelings of dislocation and the sense of instability looming all around them. In most instances, the very old and the very young were some of the first to be taken from the ghettos in these roundups, particularly when Nazi administrators were focused on maintaining an adult workforce that would provide free labour for them. In other instances, roundups by ghetto police and gendarmes would result in random people — those who happened to be in the wrong place at the wrong time — being taken to fill the deportation quotas.

Rumours were spreading in the ghettos about mysterious places with names such as Treblinka, Bełżec and Auschwitz — from which no one was known to have ever returned. To children, living with the daily uncertainty of an *Aktion* taking place must have been terrifying. Even among young children, there was an awareness that people who were being taken away by the Nazis were never coming back. As Anita writes about her parents: "Every day I was afraid until I saw them again."

For most children in this situation, childhood was over. Many parents now shifted their focus from shielding their children as much as possible to explaining what was happening so that their children would have a fighting chance to survive. Although some parents might have lost their own desire to live, they now desperately focused on making certain that their children would somehow survive. For some Jews, obtaining a "privileged" position within the German ghetto administration or making oneself useful to the Nazis was a way to attempt to save their children. Some Jews, like Anita's father, were able to reach out to Polish Catholics, whom they often came into daily contact with through their work. Debates within families broke out. Should they attempt to convince a Pole to take their child out of the ghetto? Would they have to pay to bribe people to do the right thing? Jewish parents in the ghettos across Poland had to weigh life-altering decisions: should they trust a virtual stranger to protect their child's life, or should they take the risk and keep their child with them? It was an impossible dilemma for any parent to consider.

For Polish Catholics approached by Jews for assistance, this was not an easy decision to make either, and they had to consider a request carefully. Nazi law stipulated that any person caught aiding or abetting Jews would be executed; this included sharing rations with Jews or attempting to hide them. And since the Nazis often punished entire families in order to intimidate others from saving Jews, rescuers would be putting their extended families at risk as well. Once the decision to take in a Jewish child had been made, careful planning had to follow. How could the child be smuggled out of the ghetto? Where was it safe for the rescuer to take the child? Could the child be convinced to go quietly with the Polish stranger, leaving parents and all that they knew behind? Of course, parents often had to convince their child that staying in the ghetto would mean death and that going with a stranger was the only option to stay alive. The survival odds of children who were smuggled out of the ghettos were not good, but remaining in the ghettos reduced chances of survival even more. When the Nazis invaded Poland in 1939, there were approximately 1.6 million Jewish children alive, and by the war's end, approximately 1.1 million of them had been killed. The odds were clearly working against the hidden children and their courageous rescuers.

While rescues of Jews by Poles during the Holocaust was rare, the thousands who did undertake it were often part of underground organizations, such as the aid society Żegota.[1] Rescuers formed networks, forged false identity papers giving Jewish children "Aryan" names, organized safe houses and attempted to protect their charges from roundups and death. Some rescuers, like Anita's, were operating alone without the benefit of secret organizations and material support.

Rescuers had to agree on stories that explained how a child had suddenly come to live with them. The cover story had to be plausible so that neighbours' suspicions were not raised enough to warrant a denunciation. For a hidden child, like Anita, it meant learning how to pass as a gentile child. Some Jewish children, if they did not fit the stereotyped imagery of what Jews were supposed to look like, had an opportunity to mix with the Polish community. This meant, however, that the child had to be mature enough to memorize a new name, a new family history, and, in many cases, the child had to learn how to be Catholic. This was critically important since the hidden child could be called upon to say Catholic prayers and would have to do so without hesitation. Other hidden children, who were thought to "look" Jewish, were largely confined to living inside the rescuer's

---

1   Żegota, the Council to Aid Jews, was a secret organization formed in 1942 by Polish and Jewish resistance movements and political parties with the mission to help Poland's Jewish population. Thousands of Jews were saved because of Żegota's efforts.

home, hiding whenever someone came to the door of the hο, remaining still and quiet.

Although life in the Catholic Polish household offered a degreι of safety and stability, most hidden children's lives were dominated by the fear that if they disappointed their host families they would be abandoned by them. It was especially challenging for younger hidden children who had to conceal their identities, no matter what. The stakes were simply too high, and no one could be trusted with the secret information that a Jewish child was being harboured by a Catholic Polish family. Rescuer families were often denounced by an eager neighbour, probably hoping to receive a reward of some sugar or flour (the typical reward for handing over hidden Jews). If the family was suspected, they could be terrorized by local police. Often, it became apparent to the family that it would be dangerous to continue to hide the child in their home. In some cases, like Anita's, the hidden children were returned to their parents in the ghettos. Emanuel Ringelblum, the noted historian who created an archive on the Warsaw ghetto, wrote about another such case:

*I know an eight-year-old boy who stayed for eight months on the Aryan side without his parents. The boy was hiding with friends of his father's, who treated him like their own child. The child spoke in whispers and moved as silently as a cat, so that the neighbors should not become aware of the presence of a Jewish child. He often had to listen to the antisemitic talks of young Poles who came to visit the landlord's daughters.... On one occasion he was present when the young visitors boasted that Hitler had taught the Poles how to deal with the Jews and that the remnant that survived the Nazi slaughter would be dealt with likewise... He [the boy] is now staying in a narrow, stuffy hideout, but he is happy because he is with his parents.*[2]

---

2  Emanuel Ringelblum, "Jewish Children on the Aryan Side," in *Children during the Holocaust*, by Patricia Heberer (Washington, DC: United States Holocaust Memorial Museum Center for Advanced Holocaust Studies, 2011), documents 9–10, 349.

As with children who were hidden, the notion of a stolen childhood comes into play in the ghettos, as children often weren't able to go outside, to move or to speak during the day at all. For Anita, the ghetto was clearly no longer a safe place to be, and she was once again sent away from her family. It is barely imaginable to think of parents having to separate from their child a second time after they had been reunited.

Anita's memoir reminds us of the everyday dangers hidden children faced. Like other hidden children, she could never let her true identity be known and could never let her guard down. Again, quoting from Ringelblum's notes:

*There were no problems with Jewish children as far as the need for keeping their Jewish origin secret. In the ghetto Jewish children went through stern schooling for life. [...] They ceased to be children and grew up fast, surpassing their elders in many things.... I know of a young girl who was dying in an Aryan hospital, far from her parents. She kept the secret of her origin till her death. Even in those moments of the death agony, when earthly ties are loosed and people no longer master themselves, she did not betray herself by a word or the least movement. When the nurse who was present at her death bed called her by her Jewish name, Dorka, she would not reply, for she remembered that she was only allowed to respond to the sound of the Aryan name, Ewa.*[3]

By March 1944, the region where Anita was in hiding was being liberated by the Soviet army. Many of the Soviet soldiers earned a terrible reputation, stealing whatever objects they wanted from the local people, raping women and getting drunk. For hidden children such as Anita, the war was not really over. Technically she was liberated, but how would she locate her family? Who was still alive in her extended family? And how would she, a child, go about locating them? For most hidden children, there was an additional problem:

---

3   Ibid., 350–351.

if they had been with their rescuer family for years, their biological family members might be strangers to them. Some children had converted to Catholicism in their quest to create a new identity that was as believable as it needed to be in order to survive. Should they remain with families who had cared for them and had given them a chance to live, or should they seek out long-lost family members and try to reconstruct their lives as Jews again? For many survivors, the desire to find remaining family members was of paramount importance, but hidden children did not necessarily know how to utilize primarily Jewish aid organizations to locate possible surviving family members.

As the war was drawing to a close, Poles living in areas dominated by Ukrainians were at the mercy of armed militia men roaming the streets, threatening Jews and Poles to get out of what they considered to be Ukrainian territory. Poles, after having lived under Soviet control, then German, then Soviet, then Ukrainian authorities, were forced to move westward, toward Germany. For the nationalistic Ukrainians, led by Stepan Bandera, Jews and Poles were not wanted in what they thought would be their new Ukrainian country. This led to even more upheaval in the lives of people who had endured such tragedies. For Poles and Jews from this region, it often meant undertaking a harrowing journey toward Silesia. Silesia had historically been controlled by Germans and by Poles, and now, in 1945, it was under Polish control again. In the post-war chaos, with its population transfers, redrawn boundary lines and the start of the Cold War, one can easily imagine how difficult it would be to track down potential survivors.

For so many students studying World War II and the Holocaust, there is a belief that once the war was over, life returned to some semblance of normality and the nightmarish years came to an end. However, Anita's memoir underscores the long-lasting trauma of losing the majority of her extended family. Her writing reminds us that after the war she was left to struggle with questions about her identity and to grapple with the fears that were instilled into her as such a young child. No matter how many people told her that she did not need to be afraid to be herself — Anita, a Jewish girl — that was no easy task after all of the upheavals and losses she had endured.

Anita's journey took her to Paris, then on to Canada. Throughout these post-war years of travel, Anita, like so many hidden children, had to make critical decisions about whom to trust, and the struggle to readjust and reconcile her present self with her past self was an ongoing process. Many children who survived in hiding found that their experiences were not valued: most people were not interested in hearing what it was like to be uprooted from family, left to the mercy of strangers and then left to face the future in a new, unfamiliar country, often as orphans. And yet, Anita wanted more than anything to fit in as a Canadian teenager and threw herself into her studies and her friendships, ultimately finding love and belonging in her new home. And she never lost touch with her rescuers, the family that risked their lives to save a Jewish child.

Anita Helfgott Ekstein's memoir, the story of a lost childhood and the courage to keep living, expresses hope for a better tomorrow, a world where children do not need to be hidden in order to survive.

*Beth A. Griech-Polelle*, PhD
Kurt Mayer Chair of Holocaust Studies
Pacific Lutheran University
2019

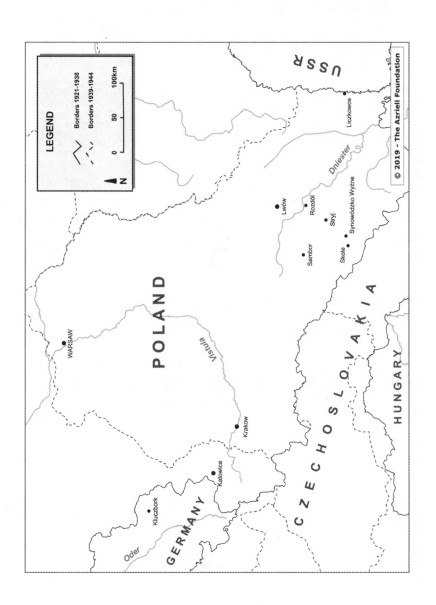

# Anita Helfgott Ekstein Family Tree

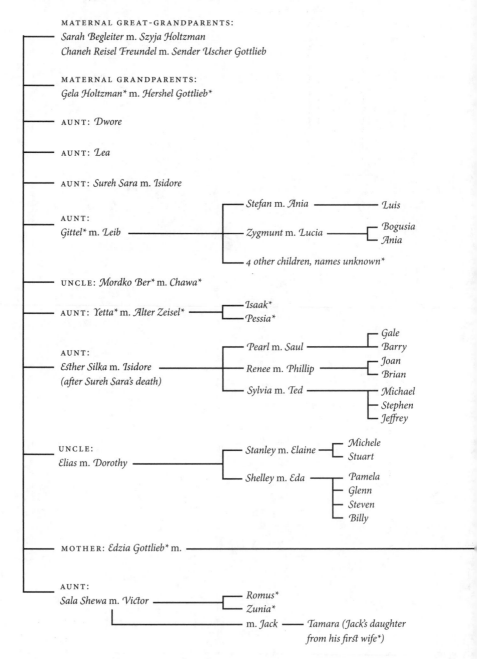

MATERNAL GREAT-GRANDPARENTS:
*Sarah Begleiter* m. *Szyja Holtzman*
*Chaneh Reisel Freundel* m. *Sender Uscher Gottlieb*

MATERNAL GRANDPARENTS:
*Gela Holtzman\* m. Hershel Gottlieb\**

AUNT: *Dwore*

AUNT: *Lea*

AUNT: *Sureh Sara* m. *Isidore*

AUNT:
*Gittel\** m. *Leib*
— *Stefan* m. *Ania* —— *Luis*
— *Zygmunt* m. *Lucia* —— *Bogusia* / *Ania*
— *4 other children, names unknown\**

UNCLE: *Mordko Ber\** m. *Chawa\**

AUNT: *Yetta\** m. *Alter Zeisel\** — *Isaak\** / *Pessia\**

AUNT:
*Esther Silka* m. *Isidore*
(after Sureh Sara's death)
— *Pearl* m. *Saul* — *Gale* / *Barry*
— *Renee* m. *Phillip* — *Joan* / *Brian*
— *Sylvia* m. *Ted* — *Michael* / *Stephen* / *Jeffrey*

UNCLE:
*Elias* m. *Dorothy*
— *Stanley* m. *Elaine* — *Michele* / *Stuart*
— *Shelley* m. *Eda* — *Pamela* / *Glenn* / *Steven* / *Billy*

MOTHER: *Edzia Gottlieb\** m.

AUNT:
*Sala Shewa* m. *Victor* — *Romus\** / *Zunia\**
— m. *Jack* — *Tamara (Jack's daughter from his first wife\*)*

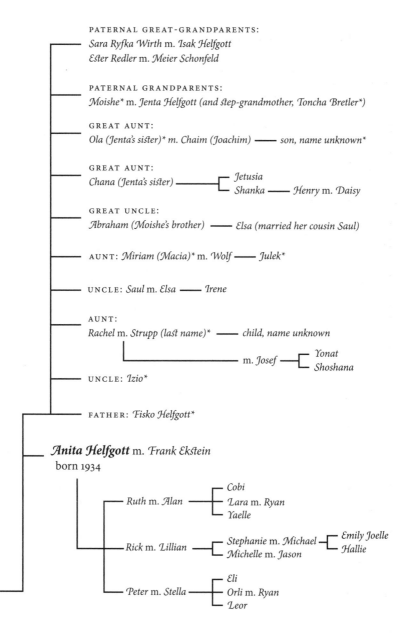

PATERNAL GREAT-GRANDPARENTS:
*Sara Ryfka Wirth* m. *Isak Helfgott*
*Ester Redler* m. *Meier Schonfeld*

PATERNAL GRANDPARENTS:
*Moishe\** m. *Jenta Helfgott (and step-grandmother, Toncha Bretler\*)*

GREAT AUNT:
*Ola (Jenta's sister)\** m. *Chaim (Joachim)* —— *son, name unknown\**

GREAT AUNT:
*Chana (Jenta's sister)* ——⌐ *Jetusia*
                   └ *Shanka* —— *Henry* m. *Daisy*

GREAT UNCLE:
*Abraham (Moishe's brother)* —— *Elsa (married her cousin Saul)*

AUNT: *Miriam (Macia)\** m. *Wolf* —— *Julek\**

UNCLE: *Saul* m. *Elsa* —— *Irene*

AUNT:
*Rachel* m. *Strupp (last name)\** —— *child, name unknown*

                           m. *Josef* ⌐ *Yonat*
                                   └ *Shoshana*

UNCLE: *Izio\**

FATHER: *Fisko Helfgott\**

**_Anita Helfgott_** m. *Frank Ekstein*
born 1934

                ⌐ *Cobi*
     *Ruth* m. *Alan* ——⊢ *Lara* m. *Ryan*
                └ *Yaelle*

     *Rick* m. *Lillian* ⌐ *Stephanie* m. *Michael* ⌐ *Emily Joelle*
                  └ *Michelle* m. *Jason* └ *Hallie*

                ⌐ *Eli*
     *Peter* m. *Stella* ——⊢ *Orli* m. *Ryan*
                └ *Leor*

**\*Murdered in
the Holocaust**

*In memory of my parents, Edzia and Fisko Helfgott, and in honour of my children and grandchildren.*

# Foreword

From my earliest memories, the Holocaust was a constant and real presence in our home. I, along with my brothers, Peter and Rick, grew up knowing that our mom was a survivor, and every event or holiday was marked by Mom's pronounced sadness over the absence of her parents. Over time we learned the details of her story and came to understand the horrors she had endured and the tremendous emotional consequences of her losses, which she combatted on a daily basis.

And yet we did not grow up in an unhappy home. On the contrary: Mom, together with Dad, filled our home with love, laughter, music, books, games and outings. It was family first — always. Mom had desperately wanted a family, and she focused her energy on providing for our needs. She ran the house without any help, provided only home-cooked meals and was significantly engaged in supporting public school education and in Jewish community work. Yet she always found time to attend our many sports and music events and loved doing so. Although money was tight during our childhood, we never felt we lacked anything. She may have gone without anything new or even a simple vacation for many years, but she found money for piano lessons, skating and hockey, Jewish summer camp, and even a baby grand piano.

Education played an important role in our lives. Mom was always available to help with homework and, being a voracious reader herself, instilled in us a passion for reading. Although neither of our parents had the opportunity to get a higher education, and Mom had to go to work before she finished high school, it was a given that we would all go to university. We understood how fortunate we were to be the first in the family to do so and took this responsibility seriously. And when Mom decided to pursue a long-desired degree and graduated from York University — at the same graduation ceremony as Peter — I was not sure who was proudest.

The other foundation of our lives was being Jewish. It was critical to Mom that, after everything she and her family had lost in the Holocaust, we would know and remember our history, grow up with a strong Jewish identity and proudly support Jewish causes and the State of Israel. Mom took us on the United Jewish Appeal (UJA) Walk with Israel event as kids and still goes to the event with our families today. She took us to rallies for Soviet Jewry, to Holocaust memorials and to community celebrations, and we watched her organize and oversee a number of Jewish causes from our kitchen table. She took us to synagogue for the holidays, created a traditional Jewish environment in our home and made sure we attended Hebrew school three times a week. She was also very clear that we were to be friends with everyone but were expected to marry Jewish partners. In 1976, days after the raid on Entebbe, Mom and Dad took us to Israel for the first time. It was a hugely meaningful experience for all of us and sparked our lifelong passion for the country.

Reflecting on our childhood as adults with our own families, my brothers and I stand in awe of our mom. This is because she did not just survive the Holocaust, she survived the surviving, and then some. She put every ounce of energy from her heart and soul into creating a wonderful life for herself, my dad and her children. She created lifelong relationships with her girlfriends, opened her heart to our extended families, realized her dream of getting a university degree and engaged in the Jewish community in a singularly spectacular way. She has chaired or been involved in many Jewish organizations, has received many awards for her accomplishments and has affected thousands of people. Mom committed herself to Holocaust education, emphasizing the importance of choosing love over hate, learning tolerance and standing up to make a difference. On one particular March of the Living trip, my daughter Lara and I accompanied Mom. As we walked silently, arms linked, surrounded by thousands of teenagers carrying Israeli flags, Mom said, tears streaking down her face, "You don't understand. I was not supposed to be here; you were not supposed to be here. None of these kids should be here. This is the proof that Hitler did not win. This is our revenge."

Sharing these experiences with my mom has made all of us appreciate the enormity of the Holocaust, the responsibility we have to educate the next generations against hate, and the need to ensure we stand up against antisemitism, intolerance and racism.

My brothers and I are incredibly proud of our mother's accomplishments, and we feel so fortunate to have her in our lives. She has had an enormous impact on us, our spouses, her eight grandchildren and two great-grandchildren. She has instilled in us a strong commitment to and love for family, being Jewish and Israel. It is extraordinary to think that a young Jewish child, orphaned and traumatized by the Holocaust, who converted to Catholicism, could one day be such a well-known figure in Jewish Toronto, where she is extremely respected, admired and loved. She has led by example and prepared us to carry on her love of teaching, community and *tzedakah*, charity. We want to say, thank you, Mom — with love, appreciation and admiration.

Mom did not just survive, she has thrived. She has shown an incredible inner strength that let her create and live an ethical, productive and meaningful life.

*Ruth Ekstein*

# Cherished

I was born on July 18, 1934, in Lwów, Poland, to Edzia and Fischel Helfgott and was raised in Synowódzko Wyżne, a small town in what was then Poland. Today, the town is called Verkhnie Synovydne and is located in western Ukraine. I am one of the only known survivors of this community.

My father Fischel, Fisko in Polish, was born on May 12, 1905, in Stryj, Poland. Located approximately forty kilometres from Lwów, Stryj's Jewish presence dated back to the sixteenth century. Historically, Jews had contributed to the local economy as trades-people, artisans and merchants. Zionism was a popular political force in the town in the late nineteenth and early twentieth centuries. By the late 1930s, Stryj's approximately twelve thousand Jews — roughly one-third of the total population — lived alongside their Ukrainian and Polish neighbours and participated in all aspects of religious and secular life. The community supported a Jewish hospital, *chevra kadisha* and a boarding school. To meet the needs of the Jewish children who attended public schools, an afternoon Hebrew language school was established.

My paternal grandfather, Mojzesz Mordko Helfgott, or Moishe, was a leading figure in Stryj. Moishe was a well-known and respected Hebrew school teacher and served as principal of the Jewish high school. Moishe and his first wife, Jenta, had three children together:

Miriam (Macia) was born in 1902; Saul, born the following year; and Fischel. Jenta died giving birth to my father, leaving Moishe alone to raise two young children and a baby. I am named for my grandmother Jenta. My grandfather's second wife, Toncha Bretler, bore him two more children, Rachel (Rela) and Izio.

As a young child, my parents and I went to visit my grandfather Moishe and my step-grandmother, Toncha. She was quite nice to me. I remember these visits well but have vague memories of my grandfather. I suppose that my memories are scant because Moishe was a bit strict, and perhaps because I saw my maternal grandfather more often and he paid more attention to me.

My mother, Edzia (Ettel Rivka) Gottlieb Helfgott grew up in the nearby town of Sambor, in present-day Ukraine. Like their Stryj brethren, Sambor's Jews had called the town home for generations and played important roles in local industry and trade. Jewish Sambor was home to various social welfare institutions, including a benevolent society, a bride's fund (to help young couples without means to prepare a wedding and set up a home), an association for the disabled and a committee that allocated funds for higher education. It also boasted a Talmud Torah, a Hebrew school, a girls' commercial school and numerous cultural and sports clubs, as well as a WIZO (Women's International Zionist Organization) branch that was founded in Sambor in 1936 and supported hundreds of children.

Edzia's father, my maternal grandfather, Hershel Gottlieb, was a very religious man and was a learned rabbi. He was very warm and used to take me for rides in his horse-drawn buggy when we visited Sambor. I remember those times with great fondness. His wife, my maternal grandmother, was Gela Holtzman. My mother was the second youngest of ten children: Dwore and Lea died at birth or shortly after, and Sureh Sara passed away when she was twenty-four. Then there was Gittel (Gela), Mordko Ber, Yetta, Esther Silka, Elias, my mother, and her younger sister, Sala Shewa, who was to play a monumental role in my life.

Education was highly valued on both sides of my family. After completing high school, Fischel went on to study accounting. In the early 1930s, he was posted as an accountant for a lumber mill company in Sambor for a while. A large company, Godula had mills all throughout eastern Poland. My mother was a very intelligent woman. She and Aunt Sala were the youngest children in the family and the only two who worked outside the home. This was a bit unusual, but times were changing and the family needed the money. The sisters both attended a commercial school and spoke six languages between them. Aunt Sala worked for a lawyer, and my mother worked for Godula as a secretary in the same office as my father. This is where they met. Edzia was several years older than Fischel. Many years later, Aunt Sala told me that while my mother was worried about the age difference, my father did not care. The two fell in love and married in Drohobycz, Poland, in 1933.

Although my parents lived and worked in Synowódzko Wyżne, I was not born there. When my mother became pregnant, the doctor warned my parents that it might be a difficult birth because she was having me a little bit later in life. The doctor told my parents to go to the big city of Lwów, about one-and-a-half hours away, where they could receive better medical care in the event that my mother needed surgery. I was born in Lwów by Caesarean section. In those days, it was a dangerous thing, a major surgery. After the surgery, the doctor told my mother that she could not have any more children. So, as you can imagine, she doted on me.

My earliest memories are of my hometown. Many of its residents, like my parents, worked for the Godula lumber mill. As a child, I thought we were one of only three Jewish families who lived in a town of several thousand inhabitants. I later found out from Freddie Segal, a resident of the town who escaped in 1941, that there were probably two hundred Jews in the town in the late 1930s.

My parents and I lived in a house on the town's main street. The house had three apartments, and to get to our apartment we had to climb a short flight of stairs at the back of the house. There were two apartments on the ground level, separated by a staircase: we lived in one, and another Jewish family occupied the other. I was friends with the little girl who lived next door. She was the same age as me, and we played together often. The family's name was Segal, but I cannot remember the girl's first name.

The Ukrainian landlord, Vasil Kamionkowie, lived above us with his wife, Paulina, and their family. I remember our apartment being quite attractive. It had a kitchen, a living/dining room with a closed-in porch and two bedrooms: my parents' room had a double bed and mine had a single white bed. Our apartment also had a bathroom with a bathtub and hot running water. This was somewhat of a luxury in those days, as was electricity. A tall tiled stove was situated in the centre of the home and heated the apartment. Our dining room had a beautiful wooden buffet with delicate engravings and a matching table and chair set. I do not recall what type of wood everything was carved from, but I remember it being dark. The large room also had some armchairs, a large white wardrobe with a mirror, and a china cabinet that held a radio. Sometimes we listened to music, and both my parents listened to the news on the radio.

There is a great deal that I do not remember about my childhood. One thing that I clearly recall, however, is that I was a terrible eater. Apparently, I didn't like to eat, and I would keep food in my cheek and refuse to swallow. Pictures of me as a little girl show that I was quite fat, but my mother didn't think I ate enough, and she wanted to feed me even when I'd had my fill. My mother worried so much about my eating that, at the age of three, I was sent to a sanatorium in Zakopane, a resort town in the Tatra Mountains. There, I was expected to "learn how to eat." Every day, the other children and I were placed outside on cots to get fresh air. Because no one there stuffed me or forced me to eat, I ate properly.

I was at the sanatorium only a short time before I became sick with a severe ear infection and had to have mastoid surgery to clear the infection. My father was notified but was afraid to tell my mother how sick I had become and that I'd needed an operation. So instead of my parents coming to visit me, he called my aunt Sala, who was then living in Krakow a short distance away from the sanatorium, and asked her to check on me. I remember waking up and seeing Aunt Sala sitting by my bed and little wooden toys on my night table. After several days, my aunt took me home, and I was reunited with my parents. The experiment of sending me to the sanatorium did not work as my parents had hoped, but my mother must have been told to let me eat only when I was hungry because she did not force-feed me anymore.

After I recovered from my surgery, I made friends with some of the children who lived in my neighbourhood. Some were Polish, some were Ukrainian. We all played nicely together outside our houses and did not think about the differences between us. We were too young for that. I also remember going to a nursery school several times a week because my mother was working. The school day was filled with games and songs and the recitation of verses, but nothing religious. And although children of all nationalities attended, most of the children were Polish and we all spoke Polish.

As a child, I was completely spoiled. My parents doted on me. I was their only child, the apple of their eye. I had my own room full of toys. I remember getting a beautiful doll that said "Mama" when you laid her down. I wanted to know how this worked, so I opened her stomach and found a box that talked when it was tilted. I cried when I realized that my doll was ruined. It was a very naughty thing to do, and while my parents did not punish me, I am sure they were unimpressed with my behaviour.

My father was a very tall man, over six feet, and my mother came up to his shoulders. He was talented and had many hobbies, including stamp collecting, and he was also an amateur photographer. As a child, he had been part of the scouts, and he remained an avid sportsman into adulthood. When I was four years old, he took me skiing for the first time, and I loved it, but my mother was worried. I remember that we had a deer head with antlers mounted on a wall in the living room. My father was quite a man.

We often went for walks through the town, with me hoisted high up onto my father's shoulders. He would also play with me and taught me many things. My aunt Rachel once wrote me a letter telling me that she remembered me sitting in the highchair and throwing a piece of bread on the floor. My father made me pick it up and kiss it because "one didn't throw bread on the floor," but he didn't chastise me or yell at me. Instead, he just told me very gently what I should do. However, most of my memories of my father are from what happened later.

From what I can remember, my mother was a little like me. People who knew her have told me that I look very much like her. I do not remember if my mother had any hobbies or special talents, besides being very gentle and kind. There is one fond memory I like to revisit. As a little girl, my mother and I would travel to Krakow to visit Aunt Sala and her family: her husband, Victor Stern, and two children, my cousins Romus and Zunia. On those visits my mother would take me downtown to watch a real human bugler on the tall tower of Saint Mary's Church. The bugler was always a highlight of my trip. Every hour on the hour, the bugler popped out of four windows to blow the bugle, facing north, south, east and west. But the bugler never finished a complete call. The legend goes that the bugler's call dates back to the Middle Ages. During the 1241 Tatar invasion, a watchman saw the enemy approaching and sounded the alarm to warn the population. Before he could finish, an arrow pierced the bugler's throat. To this day, the music always stops mid-note.

In our home, our primary language was Polish. My parents spoke Yiddish, their *mama loshen*, mother tongue, to each other when they did not want me to understand, so I never learned the language. Or maybe they spoke Polish with me because this was the dominant language in our town and because we were quite assimilated. Similarly, my grandparents spoke Polish to me but Yiddish to each other. It was probably a good thing in the long run that my Polish was fluent. Speaking perfect Polish, and no Yiddish, might have saved my life. Later, I also learned to speak Russian and Ukrainian.

Although I could not yet read, our house was full of books in many languages. My parents also spoke German and were taking French lessons before the war, and they had a group of friends that would get together to take English lessons. Somehow the memory of one word in particular, "child," sticks in my mind. I think it is because "child," sounds like the word "chai," tea, in Russian or Ukrainian. Every time I heard the word "child," I thought they were talking about tea!

I imagine my parents were learning English because they were hoping they would be able to emigrate one day. My mother's brother Elias had immigrated to the United States in the 1920s, married his wife, Dorothy, and had two children, Stanley and Shelley. And my mother's sister Esther and her family were in New York. Shortly after Esther's marriage, her husband, Isidore (Iser), had immigrated to the United States. He apparently did not know she was pregnant at the time, and would not meet his daughter, Sylvia, until seven years later, when he could afford to bring them to New York. Esther and Isidore had two more daughters once they reunited, Pearl and Renee.

I have a letter, written by my mother to her sister in New York in 1938, giving all the family news. In the letter, she mentions that things were getting difficult and that they were very worried about the situation for Jews in Poland. My mother pleads with her sister, writing that, if it was possible to acquire the necessary visas, my parents would love to immigrate to the United States. She adds that they would not be a burden, that my dad was a wonderful person who was not afraid of work.

I always knew that I was Jewish even though my mother and father were not very religious. Rather, they were traditional but worldly. My mother lit the Shabbat candles every Friday night, but I didn't have any formal Jewish education. I learned more about Judaism, and our traditions, only after the war.

I do not remember much about Jewish life in our town, and I don't recall there being a large synagogue. But I do remember going to a *shtibel*, a little synagogue, for services on Rosh Hashanah and Yom Kippur. One year, Mother fasted on Yom Kippur. We came home after many hours of prayer, and she fainted because she hadn't eaten all day. I clearly remember my dad telling her that she shouldn't fast. For holidays like Passover and for Rosh Hashanah, we often travelled to my grandparents in Sambor to be together as a family.

Although none of our relatives lived in Synowódzko Wyżne, my grandparents, aunts, uncles and many cousins lived in neighbouring towns, not too far by train, and we visited often. I loved seeing them. My father's family was about two hours away in Stryj, and my mother's family was three or four hours away in Sambor.

My grandparents on my father's side were traditional Jews but worldly and open to modern concepts. They had good relationships with non-Jews in Stryj, and Moishe, my grandfather, was well respected in the community. Moishe dressed in secular clothing and did not wear the black coat and the fur hat that my maternal grandfather wore.

While my paternal grandparents were traditional Jews, my mother's side of the family was extremely religious, strictly Orthodox. As a matter of fact, my maternal grandfather, Hershel, didn't think that modern Fischel was religious enough to marry his daughter. I understand there was a bit of a to-do about him wearing a *kittel*, the white robe that Orthodox Jewish men wear over their clothing during the marriage ceremony. Apparently, my father did not want to wear it. Eventually he was convinced to do so, satisfying his new in-laws. Years later, my cousin Stefan told me that our grandfather had presided over his marriage wearing a long black caftan and a black hat. Although my mother kept a kosher home, my grandparents never came to visit us because they didn't quite trust my father that it would be just right.

# The Horrors Begin

World War II broke out on September 1, 1939. I remember that day well. Everyone, even the children, knew that war had started. The shrill sounds of airplanes filled the air. The children were warned that the enemy planes might be dropping bombs or poisoned toys from the sky and that we should not pick up anything from the ground. There was also fear of a gas attack. My family was issued gas masks and my father brought them home.

The next thing I knew, there were Polish soldiers running by our house with their shoes in their hands. The Polish army was retreating, defeated and overrun by Hitler and the German army after only two weeks, and they were running eastward, toward the Soviet Union. I remember looking out the window and watching them run along the train tracks in front of our house.

Within two weeks, the country was occupied from the east by the Soviet army and from the west by the Germans. On August 23, 1939, German and Soviet foreign ministers had secretly signed a non-aggression treaty, better known as the Molotov-Ribbentrop Pact. Each party promised not to attack one another for a ten-year period. The pact also outlined the terms of partition into German and Soviet spheres of influence over Eastern Europe. Without fear of being stopped, the German army attacked Poland on September 1, and the Soviet army occupied and annexed eastern Poland shortly after.

Essentially split into two halves, Poland ceased to exist as before. My parents and I lived in the territory that fell under Soviet authority.

I was five years old when the Soviets took over, and life went on more or less the same for me. Both of my parents continued to work in the office of the Godula lumber company, although the mill was nationalized. Management changed, and Russian overseers replaced the Jews, Poles and Ukrainians who had previously held those roles. Luckily, unlike many other people, both my parents kept their jobs.

Soon after the Soviets took over, I began preschool in our town. Unlike in Canada, Russian children do not begin elementary school until they are seven years old, so I wouldn't be ready to start school until September 1941. Although much remained the same for me during these years, food was scarce. Every day, the teachers fed us lunch, and once, they served us spinach. I did not like spinach, and in protest, I left school and ran home. My parents were not happy, not so much about the spinach, but that I left school and came home alone. To this day, I still do not like spinach.

At the beginning of the war, my parents would talk to each other and to friends about what was going on, and I would overhear their conversations. But they did not talk to me very much about what was happening. I didn't really know what it meant that the Soviets were in our town; I only knew that we were living under occupation and were not entirely free. Eventually my parents had to talk to me and explain what was happening to us.

During the time we were under Soviet control, we were not aware of what was happening to Jews under German control in western Poland, including my aunt Sala, who was in Krakow when the war broke out. There was virtually no contact between the two parts of the divided country. Newspapers were censored, radio broadcasts were censored, even personal correspondence was censored. I remember a letter we received from Aunt Sala with a lot of blacked-out lines. It was impossible to know if my aunt was safe. I'm positive that if my father and mother had known what was going on, they would have followed the Soviet army eastward into the Soviet Union. Who could imagine the horrors that would come?

During the two years of Soviet occupation, we were still able to travel to other regions that had been occupied by the Soviets. We visited my father's family in Stryj on several occasions, spending some quality time there. In 1941, we travelled by train to spend Passover in Sambor with my maternal grandparents. My grandfather Hershel was kind and loving toward me. I loved him and was excited to celebrate Passover with him.

The preparations for the holiday were fascinating for me. My grandmother took me with her to the bakery where matzahs were being prepared. They did not come in a box as they do today. Instead, local women made the dough from scratch. I wanted to help, so my grandmother gave me a piece of dough to play with. When I asked for more, I was told that the dough should not be wasted. I cried but did not get any more.

The Passover dishes were in the attic and had to be brought down and washed. Lots of cooking ensued, and wonderful smells wafted all over the house. The family gathered around the table for the seder. There were many of us at the seder that year — aunts, uncles, cousins. My grandfather, wearing his white *kittel* and reclining on a pillow, was the king of the table and proceeded to lead the seder. Being the youngest one at the table, I asked the Four Questions. My mother had helped me memorize the words because I did not understand Hebrew, and everyone joined in. Many years later, I taught these same Four Questions to my own children, just like my mother had taught me.

We stayed in Sambor for the week of Passover. My grandfather took me to the synagogue and we rode across town on a fiacre, a small horse-drawn buggy. Across from my grandparents' home was a field where Roma (then called Gypsies) parked their caravans. I was afraid of them. At that time, children were often warned that if they were bad, the Gypsies would take them. One day, I was outside alone and someone from the Gypsy camp started walking in my direction. Before I had a chance to run into the house, my grandmother came out. She was horrified to see the Gypsy standing there. My grandmother was an extremely superstitious woman, and she was afraid that the Gypsy had given me an evil eye. She proceeded to build a fire outside and told me to jump across it. This supposedly took care of the evil eye.

I did not know it at the time, but this Passover would be the last time I saw my grandparents.

Shortly after Passover 1941, when my parents and I had returned to Synowódzko Wyżne from Sambor, there was a terrible flood in our town, and many buildings had to be boarded up. Our apartment was slightly elevated from the ground, so the water did not flood our home, but we could not leave for several days until the water receded.

～

On June 22, 1941, the German army invaded the Soviet Union in a military offensive known as Operation Barbarossa, and the Germans occupied our small town shortly after. As the Soviets prepared to flee east, my parents' boss suggested that my father and his family follow the Red Army into the Soviet Union. I remember the conversation that my parents had, how they contemplated the offer. Should they go with a child? Where to? My father did not believe the rumours about the freedom and opportunities that awaited them in the Soviet Union, and my parents decided against the move. They thought it would be unwise to go with a small child into the unknown. Synowódzko Wyżne was their home, and so they stayed. This was our last chance to escape; after this, there was nowhere to go. We did not know that Germany had broken the non-aggression pact with the Soviets and that an attack was coming. If my parents would have had any idea of what was coming, I'm sure they would have gone. But we didn't go, we waited. That was a big mistake.

It did not take long after the Soviets retreated for the horrors to begin. During a brief hiatus before the Germans arrived, local Ukrainians — awful people, many of them our neighbours, who had no respect for human life — went on a rampage against the Jewish residents of our town, carrying out a pogrom. Our Ukrainian landlord, Vasil Kamionkowie, had learned about the impending attack and warned my parents. He led us to a barn directly behind our house. We climbed up on a ladder and hid under the roof inside a hayloft from which we could see outside through a small opening between the roof and the wall of the barn. I believe that we hid in this hayloft for at least a week, maybe longer.

During the pogrom, people came into the barn during the day to do some chores, and we had to be very, very quiet and careful. I learned to be silent. The only time I could make noise was at night. Even Paulina, the landlord's wife, did not know we were there. Her husband was afraid she would discover us when she came into the barn to collect eggs. For me, as a child, it was an adventure; I was with my parents and felt safe and did not understand the danger. I do not remember exactly how my parents explained this situation to me, but they did tell me that our lives were in danger because we were Jewish and that we had no choice but to go into hiding. "This will pass," they told me, "and in a few days, we will come out and everything will be fine." I was only six years old at the time, and they tried to reassure me as much as they could.

We could not see much from our hiding place, but every night the landlord snuck us food and kept us informed about what was happening on the outside. The Ukrainians were exacting revenge on the Jews for the mistreatment they had suffered first under the Poles and then under the Soviet Union. As always, the Jews were their biggest target, and the retreat of the Soviet Union was a good excuse to kill a few of us. Our landlord told us that many people, including non-Jewish Poles, had been killed, Jewish homes had been looted, store windows broken and property destroyed. Others were beaten up and their belongings taken away. This was a big event in my life and brought home the seriousness of the situation. Thousands of Jews in the region were murdered that summer. I have no idea why my family was protected, but thanks to our landlord, our lives were spared.

When things quieted down, we left the barn and returned to our apartment. From that moment on, we lived in fear: we didn't know what the next day might bring. But as a young child, I still felt secure. I trusted my mother and father and believed that they could fix anything. I believed they knew how to handle any situation and that everything would be all right as long as we were together.

I do not remember anything about the day the Germans occupied our town, but within a short period of time, our lives changed forever. The German authorities occupied the entire region of eastern Galicia, which included Synowódzko Wyżne, Sambor and Stryj, and renamed the territory Distrikt Galizien. This district was added to the *Generalgouvernement*, General Government, in August 1941.

The Germans quickly introduced a series of anti-Jewish measures. These new laws limited our movements and our access to education. A curfew was imposed and other restrictive measures were instituted. My parents lost their jobs when the Germans took over the lumber mill, and I was prohibited from attending school. Different edicts came out daily. Our radios were confiscated, and it would be many years before I was able to listen to music comfortably again. Any newspapers that were permitted to continue publishing were heavily censored. All of us, from children over the age of five, were ordered to wear armbands identifying us as Jews. The armbands were white with a blue Star of David. They were made according to specific measurements and worn on the right arm. Anyone who failed to wear the armband was risking their life. My mother made a small armband for me.

Not too long after the occupation began, the Nazi authorities ordered the town's Jewish residents to report to a collection place to turn in their valuables. I do not recall if it was a square in the town or a hall, but I do remember standing in a long line with my parents and many others. My mother was forced to remove her gold wedding ring and put it in a basket. My father was wearing a coat with a fur collar. The German officers ripped off the fur lining and threw the coat back at him. We did not know what would happen next. Everyone was afraid.

My next vivid recollection is of one night soon after. For whatever reason, my parents must have been expecting something. Perhaps there had been a rumour of an *Aktion*, a roundup, or something to that effect. I remember the three of us sitting, completely dressed, waiting, with our suitcases packed. We were ready. Eventually there came a knock on our door. German officers yelled, "Open up!" My father opened the door and two soldiers stepped in. I believe they actually took the suitcases and threw them out the window before the one who I presume was the higher-ranking officer asked my father his name. After a brief consultation with the other officers, he then turned to my father and said, "No, not you." They did not want us — yet. We were granted a little bit of a reprieve.

My father, who was not a religious man, picked me up in his arms and made me kiss the *mezuzah* on the doorway of our apartment because our lives had been spared. The next morning, we found out what had happened. The Germans had nearly arrested us by mistake; they were actually looking for our next-door neighbours, the Segals, who had the little girl, my friend, who was the same age as me. By the time we woke up, the family was gone. We had no idea where the Germans took them but understood that they were taken away and probably killed. We never saw them again. I believe that we might have been spared because the Germans knew that my father was an accountant, a well-educated man who had skills that could be valuable to their operations.

Several days after this incident, we heard yelling and loud banging on our door in the middle of the night. This time we were told we were being moved and were given two hours to prepare. Our suitcases were still packed because my parents had expected that the time would come for us. Perhaps there was a rumour about impending deportations or somebody had tipped them off. There was nowhere to run. The only question that remained was what else should we take? My mother ran around, wondering what else she could pack. Photos? More clothes for me or them? Food? We had so little left. In the end my mother's efforts went to waste. The officers threw our suitcases out the door as we said goodbye to our home. I don't know whether any of our belongings were returned to us.

Eventually we were put on a truck with the other Jews who had survived the first roundup in our town, and on October 1, 1941, we were driven about ten kilometres away to a larger town named Skole. When the truck stopped, we had to walk into the area that was designated for Jews. My father was a strong man, and he held me in his arms and reassured me: "Everything is going to be all right."

My parents and I were assigned to a shared apartment with two other families we did not know. There were at least twelve or thirteen people living in the apartment, one family to a room. Everyone shared a kitchen and took turns preparing meals when food was available. Since we hadn't been permitted to bring furniture with us, our room was practically empty save for two beds. It was terribly crowded, and that was a drastic change for me, as I had always had my own room. I was very young and scared and did not know what was happening.

My family learned that this was a ghetto. The Skole ghetto was among the earliest ghettos to be established in the region and held Jews from surrounding towns and villages. This was how the Germans concentrated and controlled Poland's Jews. While there was no fence or barbed wire trapping us inside, there was a strict curfew we were forced to adhere to. Jews had to stay in the Jewish section and could not leave that area and freely move to other parts of the town where the conditions were better. We lived under the constant watch of armed German soldiers, although I remember very few encounters with them. I rarely left our little apartment. With the exception of a handful of my parents' friends, virtually everybody in the ghetto was a stranger to me.

Only people selected for work could leave. When the Soviets retreated, they blew up railway lines, bridges and roads to impede the Germans' advance. There was a bridge across the Stryj River that had been completely destroyed. The Germans used able-bodied Jewish men and women as slave labour to repair what the Soviets had destroyed. Every morning, most of the labourers were taken in trucks back to our hometown, Synowódzko Wyżne, to repair the bridge, road and railway lines. My mother did this manual labour daily, picking up stones and clearing roads. My father was usually taken to work for the Germans in a small office hut by the bridge.

While our parents were at work, older people looked after us children. They tried their best to keep us occupied, reading to us and letting us draw pictures and play games. I was left with a lady in our building along with some other children and some adults who were unable to work. But as conditions worsened and roundups were carried out, they all kept disappearing, and the faces of the people around me kept changing. If someone was taken from our room, somebody else moved in. While I do not remember the faces or names of our neighbours, I do remember waiting until my parents returned late each day. Before the war, I had never been separated from them for an entire day. And now, after everything that had taken place and all that I had seen, I was afraid that they would not come back. Every day I was afraid until I saw them again.

After a while there was very little to eat, and I was often hungry. My mother would scramble to find food. After her long days performing physically demanding work, she did her best to feed us as well as possible. There were several Jewish-operated stores, but with empty shelves, and we ate a lot of potatoes. I'm convinced my parents had less to eat so that I would have more. Within a short period of time it became nearly impossible to buy anything. I'd had only a few pieces of clothing with me when we arrived at the ghetto, and by the time winter came, there was no heat and we wore our outdoor clothes inside.

I don't really remember that period in the ghetto. I don't know what I did, I don't know how I spent the days, I don't know who was with me other than my parents. It's like I have blocked everything out of my memory. That is, until October 18, 1942.

# Miraculous Escapes

For a little more than a year, my parents and I languished inside the Skole ghetto. Every morning my parents went off to perform slave labour for the Nazis, and I waited for them, impatiently, to return each evening, unable to relax until they came home to me. On October 18, 1942, my mother did not report for work. My father went to work at the hut by the bridge in Synowódzko Wyżne. Sometime during the day, my mother told me that we were going to look for food. I don't know where we were going to go. Maybe to find a potato? If you had a potato, you could make a soup. That would be better than nothing.

Suddenly, my mother told me that she was going to leave me with a friend instead, and that she would come back and get me. I knew the friend and was not uncomfortable being there. Sometimes I rack my brain trying to understand the events of that day. Why did she leave me with her friend? Had she heard something might happen? Perhaps she had a feeling that it was better to leave me behind than to take me out on the streets looking for food. My mother saved my life that day. But luck was not on her side. The Nazis chose that particular day to stage an *Aktion* in our section of the ghetto. When my mother walked outside wearing the white armband with the blue Star of David, they must have seen her right away. She — along with everyone else not at work that day — was captured, loaded onto a truck and taken away. She had gone out to find some food and never came back.

While my mother was out on the streets of the ghetto, I must have fallen asleep. When I woke up at the friend's house, my father was sitting by the bed. He was crying. I had never seen my father cry before, and it scared me. He told me that my mother had been taken, and he did not know if we would see her again. My mother's friend had witnessed the *Aktion* from a window and had seen my mother being picked up. Thank God I was not looking out the window! I couldn't believe it. How can a person just disappear? We had been together only minutes before.

Maybe being a little girl who was forced from my home into that ghetto was such a traumatic change for me that I blocked out most of that time period, but I clearly remember this moment — waking up to find out that my mother was gone. Sometimes I think I'd like to remember more, and sometimes I think it's better not to. I was only eight years old. On the day of my mother's capture, the Nazis rounded up anyone they could find in the Skole ghetto, but for some reason, they never entered the house where I was staying. I had *mazel*, luck, to be left alive.

We didn't know where my mother had been taken. Nobody knew anything in our part of Poland. We had heard rumours of murder by gas. But who could believe this? The Nazis deliberately withheld information from their victims for fear of resistance or reprisal. They were the kings of deception.

After this incident, my father seemed to have lost his will to live but became desperate to protect me, his only child. He knew that if I remained in the ghetto, I would be caught in the next *Aktion*. He did not know exactly what had happened to those who were taken, but he understood that they were not coming back. We heard that the transports from our region were taken to a camp in the small town of Belżec. The rumours that circulated about the mass murders underway there were terrifying. My father no longer kept any secrets from me. Since he was desperately trying to save me, he told me exactly what was going on. I trusted my father and knew that he would do everything in his power to keep me safe.

Once the Germans realized how valuable my father's accounting skills were, they moved him into the office hut in our hometown permanently. There he came into contact with non-Jews, who were permitted to live outside the ghetto walls. My father quickly befriended a Polish Catholic man, Josef Matusiewicz, who had been brought from his town to serve as the stock-keeper.

Before the war, Josef had served as an officer in the Polish army. He was a very well-educated, intelligent man with a huge heart. Both he and my father spoke several languages and engaged in long conversations. Eventually, my father confided in Josef that he had an eight-year-old daughter. I was later told that during their conversations my father expressed an interest in Catholicism and an inclination to convert from Judaism after the war. My father asked this man, practically a stranger, to try to save my life and raise me as a Catholic. While I do not believe for a heartbeat that my father wanted to convert to a different religion, I understand fully why he might have made this declaration. My father was appealing to Josef's deep faith and would have said anything to save my life.

My father did not know where to turn or what to do after the loss of my mother. He was scared of the day when he would come home from work to find that I, too, had disappeared. But asking Josef to help me was a dangerous proposal. In German-occupied Poland, strict laws prohibited people from helping Jews in any way, including providing food rations or hiding Jews in their homes. Any person caught or even accused of helping a Jew risked their own life, as well as the lives of their family and, sometimes, communities.

When he agreed to take me, Josef knew he was violating Nazi law. Josef had not been a family friend, and I did not know him. Many years later, I learned about the night Josef told his wife that he wanted to bring a little Jewish girl into their home. He explained the situation and what he had been asked to do. Josef's adopted daughter Lusia told me that her mother, Paulina, was dismayed by the request: "Are you crazy? You're going to bring a little Jewish girl into our house? You're going to endanger our lives, you cannot do that!" I believe that Josef was an extremely courageous man and responded that God would help. They were a very religious family and fervently believed that God would help them protect me. Josef saw my father's desperation and could not look away. At tremendous personal risk, the decision was made to take me in.

My father tried to prepare me for another major change. He explained that it was very important that I understood that he could not keep me safe. Every day in the ghetto was dangerous for me. I knew that being Jewish was dangerous. My mother was already gone. I did not want to lose him, too. My father reassured me that I would live with people who would be good to me and care about me. Life would be much better for me there than it was in the ghetto. Before we had come to the ghetto, I was terribly spoiled, an only child. Needless to say, after a year in the ghetto, I was not spoiled any longer. I did not want to go. But my father made it absolutely clear that I had no choice in the matter. I had to go. Otherwise, he told me, I might die. And I had seen death in the ghetto. I am not sure if I understood at the age of eight what it meant to die, but I knew that it was final.

My father assured me that he would be fine, and that we would be together shortly. "It won't take long. Everything will be fine. I'll come and see you and I'll take you home...." He promised me everything a parent would promise an eight-year-old child. And so, when Josef Matusiewicz came to get me, I went along with him. I was petrified because I didn't really know this man, whom I had met only a handful of times. I didn't want to leave my father.

Josef Matusiewicz's position granted him special access to the otherwise restricted ghetto, and one night he was able to get into the ghetto to collect me. I had to say goodbye to my father. I clung to him and did not want to let go. When we could no longer delay the inevitable, Josef put me in a large bag and carried me out of the ghetto like I was a sack of potatoes. I was cautioned not to make any noise, not to move, not to draw any attention to myself. Years later I learned that there was a police station located right next to where we left the ghetto. I don't know how Josef managed to take me out. It really was a miracle that we were not caught.

Josef carried me in the bag some distance outside the ghetto to where he had a horse-drawn wagon waiting. He placed me in the bottom of the wagon and covered me with straw. He then drove the wagon for what seemed a long time until we arrived at our destination. Josef had brought me to his home in a neighbouring town called Rozdół, which is now Rozdil, Ukraine. Josef shared his home with his wife, Paulina, and an eighteen-year-old adopted niece, Emilia. The couple never had children of their own. They adopted Emilia, or Lusia as everyone called her, at birth along with two other orphans, a niece and a nephew. All three children were raised as their own. By 1942, the elder niece was married, and the nephew was a priest. Lusia was the only child living in the family home.

Josef and his wife were middle-class people and owned a little house. It was a one-storey home with a kitchen and three rooms that opened into one another. Paulina and Josef slept in one room, which I never saw; there was a living/dining room; and there was Lusia's bedroom. She graciously shared her room, and her bed, with me. The bed was raised high off the floor, and I was barely tall enough to climb up onto it. Although the indoor kitchen had running water and electricity, it lacked hot water. Whenever somebody wanted to take a bath, they had to drag a big tub into the kitchen and heat water on the stove. The outdoor bathroom was located close to the barn where the cow was kept. Although food was scarce for all Poles during the war, the Matusiewiczes grew their own food and had fresh milk from the cow. I arrived during the winter, so I didn't see the garden, but I heard about it.

I arrived in Rozdół shortly before Christmas 1942 with only a handful of possessions: the clothes I was wearing, a coat, a change of clothes and lace-up shoes. At some point, my rescuer approached our landlord in Synowódzko Wyżne to try to collect some of the clothing we had left behind. But despite having once saved our lives, the landlord refused to release my worthless belongings. He was a very complicated human being. The only item I had that I cared about was a small amulet in a pouch, which had once belonged to my mother. I do not know what was on the amulet, but I wore it around my neck to feel close to my mother — it was all I had left of her. Paulina took the amulet away from me, saying that it could identify me as Jewish. I already had so little, and the loss of the amulet was devastating. But there was nothing I could do about it. Many years later I saw something similar to the amulet at a synagogue museum in Krakow and thought of my mother.

Although I was upset, I had to move on. I focused on adapting to my new situation and family. That first day in my new home, there was a large Christmas tree, its branches decorated with real candles and little ornaments. For an eight-year-old child who had spent a year in the ghetto, this was like a fairy tale, a wonderful sight. All of the preparations for Christmas were very exciting. On the one hand, I didn't know what was going on and why, and I was afraid of everything. On the other hand, this was a different experience for me. I was terribly hungry, and my rescuers fed me food that I had not had in a long time. Then they put me to bed. Physically and mentally exhausted, and longing for my father, I fell asleep.

Christmas Eve was a few days later. Straw was placed in the corners of the main room and under the tablecloth to represent the manger that Jesus was born in. Wonderful cooking smells came from the kitchen. Carolers were singing outside. Snow was falling. During that time, I was so busy taking everything in that I was distracted a bit from thinking about how much I missed my mother and father. Lusia told me years later that I would get into bed every night, cover myself completely with blankets and cry. I did not want anyone to hear me, but they obviously did.

It was very important that I pass as a gentile child. The family called me Haneczka. I did not have any papers at this time to verify my identity. The story offered to neighbours was that I was another niece whose parents had died in an influenza epidemic. Since the couple had already raised three orphans, this was not a strange notion. I had to assume a completely new identity and forget who I had been. And the family immediately began to teach me how to be a Catholic.

Paulina Matusiewicz was an extremely devout religious woman who went to church every day. I was a very good child but deeply afraid of her. I think I feared that they would not keep me if I misbehaved. Since meeting other hidden children over the years, I have learned that this was a common experience: we were all very well behaved because we were afraid of being sent away (and possibly having our true identities as Jews revealed).

When I arrived in Rozdół, I did not know anything about the Catholic religion. I barely knew anything about the Jewish religion for that matter, only what I had seen at home. Before the Matusiewiczes could let me be seen by people, they had to teach me about being a Catholic. These lessons were supposed to protect me from accidentally revealing the fact that I was Jewish. Everyone was a potential enemy.

Worried about my true identity being discovered, Josef and Paulina did not allow me to leave the house, and if they expected visitors or heard anyone approaching, I was instructed to disappear and hide in another room or under a bed. Even though the neighbours believed that I was an orphaned niece, the family discouraged any contact between me and the outside world.

I was never outside by myself, and I spent almost all of my time in the house. The only exception was when my rescuers took me to church for Midnight Mass. Josef simply announced, "We're going to church." I was surprised they would allow anyone to see me. I can perfectly remember the snow crunching under my feet as we walked to church. It was so nice to be outside. The inside of the church was beautiful and decorated with flowers even though it was the dead of winter. The space was larger than the *shtibel* where my family used to attend holiday services, and it was filled with people. I didn't understand the proceedings at Mass, but though foreign to me, they were very interesting. I had never seen anything like this at synagogue services. The priest in his vestments went up and down the aisles with incense — I remember the powerful smell — and people went up to the front to take Communion. There was a manger with baby Jesus in it, and I wanted desperately to look at those little figurines. Josef hovered over me throughout Mass and prevented anyone from speaking with me. He was probably concerned they would ask me a question about the service that I, as a little Jewish girl, would be unable to answer. I was well behaved and saved all of my questions for later.

My feelings toward the Matusiewiczes, whom I referred to as Aunt and Uncle, were complicated during the war. I was mature enough to understand that they were trying to save my life, but for the devout Paulina, everything I did was a sin. She was very, very strict. She would accuse me of vanity and say that I was showing off if I combed my hair the wrong way. During my time there, Paulina never touched me. A tall and thin woman, she was completely unapproachable, and I was always afraid of getting in trouble with her. This was an unfamiliar feeling. My parents had adored me, and I had received many hugs and kisses from them, but Paulina was a much colder person. I missed my father very much. But there was nothing I could do about it. That's just how it was.

Lusia, on the other hand, was good to me. She was an absolute doll. She was very pretty and tall. Though, of course, I was little, so everyone seemed tall. Always smiling, she exuded kindness, although she also never hugged me or showed physical affection. I supposed this was just the family's way. Lusia was in school, training to be a teacher. I was her first pupil, and she showed a genuine interest in me. Since I had never been allowed to attend school, she taught me how to read and, to a lesser extent, write, in the evenings. The lessons kept my head occupied and distracted. She wasn't terribly religious at the time and was far less intimidating than her aunt.

I spent most of my days sitting in silence, eating meals that Paulina prepared for me and waiting for my reading lessons. Josef only came home on the odd weekend. His visits were always special. He was a wonderful, warm human being, and more nurturing than his wife. First of all, he spent time with me. I would sit on his lap as he told me news from my father, sometimes reading a letter from him aloud. I was always so excited to hear from my father and know that he was all right, and I was counting down the days until we could be together again.

Life continued on like this for more than a month. Then, one day in early February 1943, my world was shaken again. Lusia and I were sitting in the living room having a reading lesson when, through the window, we saw two Ukrainian policemen with rifles over their shoulders walking toward the porch. The police were coming to get me. A neighbour must have denounced me and told the Gestapo that the family was harbouring a Jew. And now they were coming to take me.

Without stopping to think, Lusia picked me up and ran with me to the back of the house. She opened a window, pushed me out into the snow and told me to run. It was a very cold winter and there was a lot of snow. I was not dressed for the outdoors and was wearing slippers on my feet. I was terrified. Where was I to go? There was an outhouse behind the house, and I ran toward it and locked the door. I stayed in there in the freezing cold for five hours, afraid to come out.

While I hid in the outhouse, I heard a repetitive noise in the distance. I had no idea what it was. Later, I found out that, on that day, the Germans and their Ukrainian helpers rounded up all the Jews left in Rozdół. The group was marched to the cemetery, lined up and shot. From my hiding space, I was hearing gunshots. Had the police found me, I would have been one of those shot. In the meantime, the policemen went through the house searching for me. Apparently, they turned the whole place upside down — looking under the beds, in the cupboards, everywhere. My rescuers insisted that I had gone to visit other family members and adamantly denied the claim that I was Jewish. It was a miracle that the police did not look out the window. Had they done so, they would have seen small footsteps in the snow leading to the outhouse.

It's amazing how many escapes I had. I guess I was meant to survive.

I finally crept back to the house when it was dark and quiet. Everyone was surprised to see me. They thought that the police had caught me. It turned out that a neighbour had indeed gone to the police with the suspicion that the Matusiewiczes' orphaned niece was actually Jewish. He or she had seen me in and around the house, or perhaps at Christmas Mass. Denouncers received rewards like a pound of sugar or a bottle of alcohol in exchange for information. Imagine a world where a pound of supplies is valued more than a human life.

It was impossible for the family to keep me after this. They were rightfully afraid that the policemen would come back and that, the next time, nobody would escape. Much later, I learned that the police did in fact return several times. Paulina contacted her husband and told him to move me quickly. Because of his position, Josef had access to the Hochtief compound, where my father was, and he returned me to my father in the same wagon we had used to escape the ghetto.

# A Lonely Existence

By the time I left the Matusiewiczes' home, the Skole ghetto had been liquidated, and its approximately two thousand Jewish inhabitants — nearly the entirely ghetto population — had been murdered, deported or confined in forced labour camps. Only thirty men, my father included, were temporarily spared to continue their work for the Germans in Synowódzko Wyżne building the Radom-Lublin railway. The men lived in a small compound at the Hochtief slave labour camp, established and overseen by the Munich-based Hochtief construction company. The company remains in operation today.

Conditions at the camp were horrible. The camp consisted of several little houses in a circular formation, surrounded by a fence. There was also a larger building with several rooms. I was hidden in one of these rooms. An SS officer named Stahelberger oversaw the camp's operations, and labourers faced terrible hunger, cramped and unhygienic living quarters and maltreatment by the guards. I never saw the camp during the light of day so any knowledge of its appearance and function came after the war.

My reunion with my father was a joyful one. I was so happy to see him! He hugged and kissed me and held me tight. I did not realize how afraid he was for me — I only cared that we were together once again. Of course, as a parent I can now imagine what torment he must have gone through knowing he had to protect me in such a place. He did not know how he would feed me, and he knew that I could be discovered at any moment. Two Jewish men shared the room I was in, and I vaguely recall being introduced to them. I believe one was named Artek. He and my father were apparently close friends.

At night, I slept with my father on a small cot in his shared room, and when he left for work each morning, I was placed in a wardrobe for the day. The wardrobe was a narrow piece of furniture used for hanging clothes, and my father punched holes in the back of it so that there would be enough air for me to breathe. I was not locked in but had to promise not to come out or stand by the window as there were no curtains on it. My father repeatedly warned me to be safe — at any point, people could walk into the room and discover me. One time, I left the wardrobe and stood in front of the window, looking out. It was a beautiful day and the sun was shining. I was only eight years old and could not comprehend how dangerous this act was. A Jewish labourer saw me through the window and told my father. I was terribly lucky that it was not a German soldier or officer who saw me. My father begged me to never do this again.

I don't know how I remained in the cramped wardrobe all day for seven weeks. That experience left me claustrophobic for years, and to this day I hate closed-in places like elevators. Each day I waited in the wardrobe to hear my father calling to me when he returned from work. In the evenings, he brought me whatever food he could scrounge up. Most likely the food — a piece of bread or a small bowl of soup — came from his own meagre rations. My father probably went hungry to keep me fed. Or, perhaps the food came from Josef.

One day, while inside the wardrobe, I heard the door open and something heavy landed in the room. I was so scared I could barely breathe. I heard the door close again but was afraid to look, and I'm happy I didn't. When my father returned, he was horrified to see the body of a man lying on the floor. Only after the body was removed did my father announce that I could come out of my hiding place.

Those seven weeks were terrible for both of us. My father never knew if he would find me alive when he came home from work. As for me, I was terrified the entire time until I saw my father again. Every sound, every footstep outside the door, scared me. The days were terribly long. I was a little girl, and I had nothing to play with and no one to talk to. All I did was wait for the day to end so that I could see my father again. It was miraculous that after that day at the window, and with all the soldiers and labourers coming in and out of the room regularly, nobody found me. I was extremely lucky.

In the meantime, Josef was feverishly trying to find a safer hiding place for me. He commissioned a parish priest to forge a birth certificate that granted me a new identity as a Polish Catholic girl. In a flash, I became Anna Jaworska, daughter of Jana and Edward. The certificate was dated August 15, 1935. Everything on the certificate was falsified except one item: my birthday, July 18, 1934. Nothing was shared with me about the transaction, and I don't know if the priest received payment for the document. It's possible that Anna Jaworska was a real person who had passed away and that the priest had, in a sense, reissued her identity. Or perhaps the priest made up the name for the birth certificate because my rescuers called me Anna. I doubt I will ever know the truth about the certificate's origins.

With this piece of paper, I had an acceptable identity — albeit a false one — and could travel. My father explained to me that, to stay safe, I once again needed to leave with Josef. He told me that I must do whatever I was told to do and that he would be proud of me always. "But," he cautioned, "be good, be independent and always re-member who you are." He promised that we would be together again soon, and I believed him. It was so difficult to say goodbye, and we both cried. I don't know where my father found the courage to give up his only child, not once but twice. It must have been so terrible for him, but he saved my life. I had no way of knowing this would be the last time we would see each other.

Josef returned to Hochtief very late one evening in April 1943 to sneak me out of the camp. Luck was on our side — it was a dark, starless night, and nobody saw us as we walked to the train station. When the train came, we boarded and discovered it was packed with civilians and German soldiers. There were no seats. Josef put my bag on the floor and told me to lie down on it and go to sleep, and if I could not fall asleep, I should pretend that I was sleeping so that nobody would speak to me or ask questions. It was wartime and trains did not run smoothly. I cannot remember exactly how long it took us to get where we were going, but it seemed to me a very long time. It was also an extremely tense trip for both Josef and me: had anyone closely examined my birth certificate, they might have discovered it was forged and removed us from the train, or worse.

Josef took me to a little village called Liczkowce (now Lychkivtsi, Ukraine), near the town of Husiatyn, close to the Soviet border. He felt it would be safer for me to hide in this primitive village with his nephew, who was a Catholic parish priest. Josef and Paulina had raised him and his sister because their parents had died in a flu epidemic when they were very young. The priest's name was Father Michal Kujata. I suppose that because Josef and Paulina had been so good to him, the priest could not refuse his uncle's request for help. Josef stayed for a day and then left me with two strangers: Father Michal and a housekeeper, whom I called Pani Karola.[1] I was supposedly the priest's niece.

Pani Karola had no idea that I was Jewish. Father Michal warned me to never reveal my true identity because Pani Karola was a terrible antisemite and would turn us into the authorities. She would say negative things about Jews in my presence, and I was afraid of her and believe the priest was too. I slept with her in a single bed and I was constantly on guard, worried that I might say something in my sleep. She fed me and looked after me because Father Michal was her

---

1   The word Pani is an honorific, a term of respect, used in Poland, Ukraine and elsewhere.

boss and instructed her to do so. But she never wanted me there and was a very mean, strict woman. She beat me whenever she had the chance and sometimes withheld food as punishment for the smallest transgression.

Life was very hard. Priests are by no means rich at any time, and this was wartime. However, despite general food shortages in the area, I was never hungry while I was at the parish. There was a small garden and a cow, and we existed on produce from the garden and milk from the cow, as well as on homemade butter and buttermilk. The parsonage also had a few chickens and geese, so we had eggs and chicken or goose occasionally. But while I did not want for food, I was very hungry for human warmth.

Father Michal took over my religious education. I did not know the difference between the Old Testament and the New Testament until I began to study the Bible with him. Only then did I begin to recognize the differences between Judaism and Catholicism. For instance, I learned that Catholics did not celebrate Passover or Yom Kippur, but instead had their own holidays. Religion was drummed into me from morning to night. The priest prepared me for confirmation but had little to do with me otherwise. Father Michal had no idea how to deal with a child. As a Catholic priest, he was expected to remain celibate and never marry — he was married to God. Although he was very kind, Father Michal never spoke to me in private, never asked how I was. I had nobody to talk to. It was a very lonely existence.

Aside from his role in the church, Father Michal was also a hobby photographer. Since few villagers owned or knew how to operate a camera, my protector was in high demand. Women (and later, Russian soldiers) would come by to have their portraits taken. He also captured special occasions in the parish, and my daily life, on film. Many years later, Lusia sent me several photos documenting my time in hiding.

During my time in Liczkowce, I never attended school as there was too great a risk that I might accidentally give myself away. The village was so quiet and primitive — Father Michal's congregation was mainly peasants, old babushkas with shmatas over their heads — that nobody cared who I was. However, thanks to Lusia, I was an avid reader. The only reading materials at the parsonage were stories from the Bible and books about saints. I read whatever I could get my hands on, and since we did not have electricity, I would read until the darkness arrived and signalled bedtime.

Each day I was given a list of chores to complete, including feeding the chickens. But my primary responsibility was looking after the brown-and-white milking cow — my nemesis! During the spring and summer months, I would take her out to a field and watch her graze for hours. That cow gave me a terrible time. Because the field had no fences, I had to stand beside the cow at all times. When she moved, I moved. That cow was a rotten one. She would run; every time I turned around, she was gone. One time she ventured into a neighbour's cabbage patch and destroyed the crop. The otherwise kind priest blamed me for this misadventure. For my punishment, he made me kneel on raw kernels of corn for what seemed like forever. It hurt my knees so badly! But that experience also made me tougher. After that, the priest attached a log to a chain that was around the cow's neck, so if she took off, the log would slow her down. The one and only time I milked the cow, she kicked the bucket over and all of the milk spilled out! That was the end of that chore. I hated that cow with a passion.

Despite my hatred for the cow, it was thanks to her that our stomachs stayed full. Pani Karola taught me how to churn butter, spin flax and stuff geese. This kept me very busy. Pani prepared our meals, and we ate a lot of kasha, boiled potatoes and pierogis. I can't stand the taste of kasha to this day. On special occasions, Pani would kill a chicken. I also remember a pig. I don't know if they killed it themselves or bought it, but I do recall eating the salami we made from it. It was delicious and so different from the food I had enjoyed with my parents.

Everything about my parish life stood in stark contrast to my pre-war existence. I went barefoot in the summer like the other children looking after their cows and had only one pair of shoes. As my feet grew, the shoes had to be opened in the front and tied with a string around my toes. In the fall, when potatoes had been taken out of the ground, the other children and I would find the odd potatoes left in the earth. We would make a fire and roast them. They tasted delicious.

I avoided getting too friendly with the other children because I was worried that they would discover my true identity. On one occasion I slipped, and I confided in a little girl who lived close to the parsonage. Although nothing happened, I lived in terror: Why did I tell her? What was going to become of me? Either she did not believe me, or she shared my story with her parents and they kept my secret — perhaps they were good people. Maybe someone was looking out for me. We never discussed it again, and I avoided all other close interactions with the local children.

The priest's house was located next to the parish church and cemetery, and when it got dark, I was afraid to go outside to use the outhouse. So Father Michal, wanting to show me that there was nothing to be afraid of, took me to the cemetery, to a large vault where someone had been buried. But although there was nothing to see inside the vault, living next to the cemetery still frightened me.

During my time at the parish, my biggest pleasure came in the summer, when I would climb a cherry tree in the orchard. High above the ground, I would eat cherries until I thought my stomach would burst! This was a nice memory of my time at the parsonage. I still love cherries today.

While I was at the parish, I came down with several childhood diseases: measles, mumps, whooping cough. Nobody looked after me or took me to see a doctor. During the day, Pani would put two chairs together in the kitchen and lay some type of mat on them, and I would lie on that all day while I was sick so that she could keep an eye on me. I don't know how I survived. The worst part, however, was the fact that I was dirty. There was no sink or indoor plumbing, and our water came from an outdoor pump. Once in a blue moon, a tub was brought in, water was heated and I had a bath. I had very few clothes, and these were washed in the same tub. Everything was covered in lice, and I was constantly scratching. Pani regularly put kerosene on a rag and wound it around my head to kill the lice. It did little good.

While I was living with Father Michal, an event occurred that really scared me. We were walking in the village, and I saw two people hanging from a tree. Around their necks was a sign: "I helped a Jew." I realized then that the Matusiewicz family and Father Michal were in real danger because of me.

All this time I had no news of my father. There were no letters. It is conceivable that Josef wrote to the priest to tell him what had happened to my father, but I was not told anything. I only knew that I was constantly frightened that somebody would discover my true identity. I lived from day to day, hoping and dreaming and fantasizing that one day there would be a knock on the door and my father would be standing there.

Catholicism did not mean much to me when I arrived at the parish. I studied with the priest because I had to, but I did not believe. But slowly, as time went on, I began to cling tightly to my faith, and I became a devout Catholic. I believed fervently in Jesus, and I would pray to him to make everything good again and reunite me and my father after the war. In a way, my strong faith helped me by giving me hope for the future.

To give Father Michal credit, he never baptized me. Father Michal was not the only priest to act righteously in this way. When the future Pope John Paul II was asked to baptize a Jewish child who had been hidden during the war, he advised the Catholic rescuers to delay baptizing the child in case Jewish relatives had survived.

But for the sake of appearances, I still had to kneel outside the confessional, confessing my sins. Except my only sin was messing up with that stupid cow.

When I said goodbye to my father the second time, one of the last things he said to me was, "You have to do whatever they tell you to in order to survive." I understood from my year in the ghetto how dangerous it was to be outwardly Jewish, and I trusted that practising Catholicism would protect me until the war ended. But no matter what happened to me, I never forgot who I was.

~

On March 24, 1944, the Soviets arrived in our parish. The Red Army had pushed the Germans out of the Soviet Union after terrible fighting and an over two-year siege of Leningrad, during which approximately a million Russians died because of hunger, starvation and cold. They had a terrible time pushing the Germans west. The parsonage was high above a river where women washed clothes in the summer. Now we watched the Russian soldiers crossing the river on foot and in trucks, pushing broken-down wagons, moving in a seemingly endless convoy. They didn't look like an army; they looked bedraggled and tired. I don't remember rejoicing or any kind of celebration. The villagers just stood and watched the procession. Nobody could help but wonder what problems would follow this turn of events.

When the Red Army entered the village, they became very rowdy. They were drunk and noisy, singing loudly and entering homes without knocking. Some demanded food but most preferred to steal more valuable items: watches, clocks, whatever appealed to them. One day a Russian soldier came into the parsonage kitchen when Pani Karola and I were home alone and exposed himself. I don't know what would have happened if Father Michal had not arrived just then. We had heard that many women and girls had been raped by the Soviets. I did not understand what that meant and was very shocked and frightened by this incident.

For the second time, I was under Soviet occupation as the war continued to rage in the rest of Poland. I remembered that the Soviets had not harmed us before and imagined I was free. Father Michal reminded me not to say anything about who I was, especially not to Pani Karola, whom he knew to be a terrible person. He was an angel to me, a wise man and always on the alert. As far as I know, the housekeeper never knew she helped harbour a Jewish child. Had she known my true identity, I would have been dead.

Unfortunately, Pani Karola was not the only antisemite in the parish. The war was not over yet, and the threat of violence was still real. It took quite a while until the Soviets reached Rozdół, where the Matusiewiczes lived. All this time I heard nothing from them.

On April 28, 1944, a young female soldier from the Soviet army came to the parish. She had been sent by the Matusiewicz family with a letter explaining that she had come to collect me. As a soldier it was safer for her to travel. When we were out of earshot, the soldier shocked me by saying, "It's okay, I'm Jewish." She said I no longer had to be afraid of people knowing my real religion. I was very happy to leave with her and wish I could recall her name. Father Michal willingly handed me over — what was he going to do with a little kid?

It took us quite some time to travel back to the Matusiewiczes. Everything on our journey was pure chaos. Trucks, hordes of children, old people and Russian soldiers clogged the roads with pushcarts and wheelbarrows. Everybody was on the move, and there was little motorized transportation to speak of. The soldier who accompanied me organized rides on wagons and trucks, mostly with soldiers. Along the way we slept by the roadside with other travellers.

The soldier and I stopped briefly in Tarnopol to stay with people whom she knew. Our next official stop was in Lwów, and then we arrived in Rozdół. I was so happy to see Paulina and Lusia again. Being with them I did not have to be afraid, as they knew who I was, and I was able to relax for the first time in such a long time. Unfortunately, Josef was not there when we arrived. He had been identified as a collaborator by the Soviets because he had worked for the Germans and was summarily arrested and deported to Siberia. The poverty in postwar Rozdół was unbelievable. There was no food and no clothing, as the Soviets had looted the city. In that respect, they were no better than the Germans. But they did not kill Jews. I no longer felt my life was under constant threat.

To Paulina's delight, I was now a devout Catholic and prayed often that God would unite me with my father. I still hoped that he and Josef were alive.

# Into the Unknown

As I settled back in with Paulina and Lusia in Rozdół, the Soviet front was moving west and the Allies were moving east. On May 8, 1945, the war in Europe finally ended, but there were no celebrations in our town. Although we were technically liberated, our troubles were far from over. Poles had experienced mass trauma during the war. First the Soviets had invaded, then the Germans and finally the Soviets again. Five million Polish citizens were murdered during those years: three million Jews, two million non-Jews. Hitler wanted all Poles gone and left everything in the country in ruins.

Even after the war, Polish citizens received terrible treatment. An armed faction of the Organization of Ukrainian Nationalists, known as the Ukrainian Insurgent Army, or Banderowcy, operating under the leadership of Stepan Bandera, continued to commit violence against the Poles. With their nationalistic vision of an independent, ethnically pure Ukraine, the militia group wanted the Poles gone. Militia roamed the streets, creating nights full of terror. The Polish population was terrorized and was pressured to leave the territory granted to Ukraine and repatriate to Polish lands. Civilians were tortured and murdered. No one knew when the Ukrainian militia would come or who would be next. I saw people hanged from balconies and lampposts, bodies on the street…so many dead bodies! If you didn't get out, they killed you.

By this time, I knew that my father was dead, but Paulina and Lusia refused to provide details about what happened to him. I prayed that Josef would return and tell me what he knew. But instead, nearly every day another family from Rozdół departed for the west. Eventually, our turn came. There was a knock at our door and orders came from the Ukrainian militia to leave within twenty-four hours. The three of us — Paulina, Lusia and I, not quite eleven years old at the time — were evacuated from Rozdół in June 1945. Most of the other evacuees were also female since many of the men were still in camps, or they were missing or dead. We packed our meagre belongings and loaded them onto a train with our cow. The train was similar to the cattle cars that had transported Jews to their deaths, but our conditions were completely different: we were free but had no clue what we were travelling toward. Several families, with their animals and furniture, were packed into each car. The train was slow and stopped frequently at railroad sidings, often for a few days at a time. Then the engineers would attach a locomotive and pull the railcars several more kilometres. At each stop, children would run outside to cut grass for the animals and scavenge in nearby orchards for apples or whatever grew in the ground. The adults would bring out kerosene stoves and cook meals. The journey lasted about six weeks.

When we stopped at the Stryj railway station, I asked Lusia to accompany me to my paternal grandparents' home. I knew the route from the station since my parents and I had visited often, and I knew it was only three stations from Synowódzko Wyżne. We found the apartment building and I asked the tenants if they knew what had happened to the Helfgotts. I learned that my grandfather and grandmother were murdered in 1942 and 1943, respectively. I also asked about my father's sister Miriam (Macia) Popper, a pharmacist, and her family. They were all gone. Many years later, my aunt Rachel revealed that when the Germans were taking Miriam and her family away on August 17, 1943, she gave her son, Julek, a cyanide pill and took one herself.

Some former neighbours told me that there were no Jews left in Stryj, and I believed them. How could I have known differently? Unfortunately, I did not know about the handful of relatives that had never left the town. My father's half-sister, Rachel, survived the war hidden in Stryj, as did my paternal grandmother's sister Chana Kupferberg and her daughters Jetusia and Shanka. Chana and her daughters were living in Stryj when I passed through, but I did not know that there were Jewish communal service offices where survivors could register and locate surviving relatives. I was so young and could not imagine such things. If I had known, I would have been reunited with family much earlier. Instead, I believed the neighbours' assertions that everyone had been killed. It was a wonderful surprise to later learn that Chana, Jetusia and Shanka had survived and eventually immigrated to Australia. We have maintained a relationship our entire adult lives, and we saw each other when my husband and I visited Australia. Chana and Jetusia passed away a few years ago. Shanka is now ninety-nine years old and still plays bridge. Shanka's son, Henry, is a doctor, and his wife, Daisy, and I keep in touch and saw each other when she travelled to Toronto for work.

On July 22, 1945, after six weeks of travelling, we arrived at our final destination. Kluczbork was a Silesian town located in what had been Germany before the war. The territory was now partitioned to Poland and filled with displaced Poles like us. There we received a very small house that had previously belonged to a German family. It was a single-storey home with three rooms plus a kitchen. Lusia and I shared one room, Paulina slept in another and there was a living/dining room. We had a barn for the cow and started a little garden to grow our own food, which meant that we never starved. Our nearest water source was a block away, so I had to carry many pails of water. Paulina, Lusia and I settled in and waited for Josef to return.

There was a shortage of everything. Our homes used coal for heat instead of wood-burning fireplaces or furnaces, but it was hard to come by. Our new house was near railway tracks that trains regularly passed through. Occasionally a train would stop to refuel, and we children would climb on top of the railcars and throw down as much coal as possible. There wasn't much to steal as there was a severe coal shortage after the war. The railcars were probably half-full by the time we finished with them. Fortunately, we were very fast and were never caught! When the trains left, we ran around with baskets to collect our bounty. I was a thief at the age of eleven, and it didn't bother me at all.

At home, Paulina was growing increasingly controlling of Lusia's activities, driving Lusia to sneak out of the house at night. When she got caught, I had to pretend that I hadn't known her whereabouts. Lusia had so little freedom, and it was hard for her to stand up to Paulina, who forbade her from marrying a man she had fallen in love with, ending that relationship.

By some miracle, Josef finally reunited with us. He travelled first to the family home in Rozdół and was told by neighbours that we had left. Somehow, he found us in Kluczbork. One day he just walked into our new home, very skinny and ill and barely able to walk. He had been starved in Siberia, and his recovery took a long time. Around this time details began to circulate about the fate of Poland's Jews. We heard and read about Auschwitz, Treblinka, Majdanek and the other horrors. Newspapers and radios were full of information. It is hard to believe that during the war we knew nothing about all this. We only knew what was happening in our immediate area.

I was anxious to know what had happened to my father. Josef told me that he had witnessed my father's death near the Hochtief labour camp in July 1943 but refused to tell me any of the details. I was told that I had no family left and that I would continue to stay with them. This upset me terribly. I had hoped and prayed that my father would survive and that I would be reunited with him. There had been no time to grieve before — it was just a matter of survival. Now, I was officially an orphan, and I could finally grieve openly for both of my parents.

Josef and Paulina told me that in order to remain with them, I needed to be baptized. By then I had been a practising Catholic for two and a half years, and I attended church regularly. I could not object. I realized that all my praying had not helped: my father had not survived. But I still believed in God. When I was baptized, I received First Communion and became a full-fledged Catholic. Paulina was still very religious; she prayed a lot and went to church twice a day and she wanted me to do the same. By this time, I probably believed as much as she did.

I cannot recall anything about my first day of school. My Jewish identity was still hidden, and I was afraid of getting too close to the other children. At this point, nobody explicitly instructed me to continue concealing my Jewishness; I simply understood that so long as I was in the care of Paulina and Josef, I was their orphaned niece Anna Jaworska. I have no idea whether there were other Jewish survivors in Kluczbork. In any case, my rescuers would not have permitted me to associate with them. So instead of making friends, I focused my energy on my education. I loved every minute in the classroom. Lusia had taught me how to read, and I had read (and reread) all the Bible stories at Father Michal's. I could not get enough of learning or books and devoured whatever I could put my hands on. Despite not knowing anything about math or science, I was not too far behind my classmates.

Unbeknownst to me, one month before he was murdered, my father had left a single letter with Josef. Dated June 1943 and addressed to his brother Saul Helfgott, a mining engineer in the Belgian Congo, and his wife, Elsa, the letter reads as follows:

*My Dear Saul and Dear Elsa:*

*In the hope that God at least kept the three of you* [he is including their daughter, Irene] *alive, I leave with my beloved daughter, Anita, this letter directed to you, with which, in case of need, she can come under your care. My dearest Edzia was taken eight months ago. Anita was then taken into the care of most worthy and decent people, whom only God can repay because I cannot. I am writing these words uncertain what the day or hour might bring. It will help me and make it easier for me to know that if I am no longer here, my dearest innocent child will not be left without care. I have no doubt, my dears, that you will do everything to take care of her as your own. I beg of you to help her to grow up to be an honest and decent person of worth, and God will reward you. I hope that these few words suffice. I wish you all the very best.*

*Regards,*

*Fisko*

The letter contained the last-known addresses of several relatives: Saul and Elsa in the Belgian Congo; my maternal aunt Esther Begleiter, in Brooklyn, New York; another maternal aunt, Sala Stern, in Krakow; and my paternal aunt Miriam Popper, in Stryj. At the bottom, he wrote my birthdate and place: July 18, 1934, in Lwów, Poland. The letter also contained a roster of all household and personal items entrusted to our Ukrainian landlords, Vasil and Paulina, before we were shipped off to the Skole ghetto: photo albums, my father's extensive stamp collection, clothing and some pieces of furniture.

Josef had promised my father that he would let my relatives know if I survived. In retrospect, it is amazing that my father had the foresight to leave his relatives' addresses with Josef. Being the moral and caring man that he was, Josef kept his promise and mailed postcards to my relatives. He did not have to do it: nobody knew I was alive, and he and Paulina could have just as easily kept me. But Josef was not that kind of man and absolutely did the righteous — and selfless — thing.

It took two months for the postcard to travel to New York by boat, and by the time it reached my aunt Esther, she was already aware that her sister Sala was alive and living in Katowice, Poland. Esther immediately sent a telegram to Sala, letting her know that I was alive and where I was. For an entire year, Sala had lived in Katowice, just one hundred kilometres away, unaware of my existence. Aunt Sala had lost everybody: her husband, Victor, had been sent to the east with the Polish army to fight alongside the Soviets and never returned. Her two children, my cousins Romus and Zunia, were left in the care of Victor's sister while Sala was at work. One day Sala came home and discovered they were gone.

Sala survived the Krakow ghetto and the Plaszow concentration camp, which was overseen by the notoriously cruel commandant Amon Göth, and was rescued by the German industrialist Oskar Schindler. Shortly after the Nazi invasion of Poland, Schindler, an ethnic German and a Catholic, relocated to Krakow from his native Czechoslovakia to capitalize on the German program to "Aryanize" Jewish homes and businesses. Schindler purchased a Jewish-owned enamelware business and rebranded it as the Deutsche Emalwarenfabrik Oskar Schindler (German Enamelware Factory Oskar Schindler), also known as Emalia. The factory employed at least a thousand Jewish forced labourers until it was incorporated into the Plaszow concentration camp system in late 1944. When he heard that all the inmates would be deported to death camps, Schindler reopened his factory in Brünnlitz, Moravia, as an armaments factory. Pleading to protect his workers, who he claimed were valuable for the war effort, Schindler had his assistant draw up the so-called Schindler's list, naming more than a thousand Jewish prisoners required to work in the factory, and Schindler was permitted to move his labour supply. Aunt Sala told me that en route to Brünnlitz the women's transport was detoured to Auschwitz. The women were terrified when they were sent to the showers, believing they were going to be killed, until water — not poisonous gas — came out. Miraculously, Schindler was able to rescue the women and brought them to Brünnlitz. Although Schindler's factory had purportedly become an armaments manufacturer, nearly no weapons were produced in the final months of the war. My aunt secured a job in the factory kitchen and grew to know the industrialist quite well.

After liberation, Aunt Sala returned to her Krakow apartment and found her previous landlady living there. Sala was told that since her family had not paid rent in several years, the apartment no longer belonged to them. She was not allowed to retrieve any of her family's possessions. Despondent, Sala reunited with the son of her sister Gittel, my cousin Zygmunt Horszowski, who had survived on false papers, and moved in with his family in Katowice.

On April 1, 1946, Zygmunt sent Sala with a car and driver to collect me in Kluczbork. When I came home from school that day, Lusia was waiting for me on the street and there was a car in front of our house, something that had never happened before. I wondered whose car it was. Lusia told me that my aunt was inside, but I did not believe her. I thought it was an April Fool's Day joke. I went inside and immediately recognized my aunt. My mother and I used to visit her in Krakow often, and we spent the last summer before the war together in the Carpathian Mountains. Aunt Sala had also been there when I woke up after my ear surgery in Zakopane. I was so happy to see her — I had family, someone I remembered. But Aunt Sala was so emotional, hugging me tight and crying, that she scared me half to death!

My aunt refused to return to Katowice without me, but I was reluctant to leave the Matusiewiczes, with whom I had been for such a long time. They, in turn, were unhappy about giving me up. I was torn in two directions: rescuers versus family, Catholic versus Jewish. I was terrified to leave. Who could have guessed how much my life would change yet again?

# Afraid to Be Jewish

During the long years spent away from my family, so much had changed, and I think that when Sala showed up I was in shock to discover that there were other members of my family who had survived. Josef assured me that others had indeed survived the war, and I trusted him completely. And so, after careful consideration, I agreed to return with my aunt on the condition that Josef joined us. He agreed, and I left my few belongings at the Matusiewiczes' house because I expected to return. Being driven to my cousin Zygmunt's apartment in Katowice was a novel experience for me. Zygmunt and his wife, Lucia, had survived the war on "Aryan" papers under the name of Bogusz, and they kept the name after liberation. They had a six-year-old daughter, Bogusia, and another child on the way. Josef stayed with my relatives for a few days and then returned home once I felt comfortable enough to stay. After the years in hiding, I was finally with family again. It was all so new, and I missed the Matusiewicz family a lot. Zygmunt's brother, Stefan, another surviving relative, offered Josef a small amount of money for his family. Life was very difficult for them after the war, and they had been wonderful to me. But proud Josef declined.

A couple of weeks after Josef returned home, my family expanded again. My cousin Ania was born in the apartment while I was there. The adults locked Bogusia and me in a room to prevent us from watching the birth. We heard noises and tried to look through a key-hole to catch a glimpse of the action, but we couldn't see anything. I was unhappy being locked in a room once again. On a happier note, this was the first time I saw a baby. Bogusia and I still laugh about this night whenever we meet.

On our reunion, my aunt told me that I could now leave behind the identity and nickname the Matusiewiczes gave me. I will never forget what she said: "Now you're Anita, not Haneczka. You can be who you are. There is no need to hide any longer." But I was still afraid to be Jewish. Once I was settled in, Aunt Sala took me clothes shopping to replace the old and patched pieces I had left at the Matusiewiczes. She also bought me a brand-new pair of shoes with a low heel and hooks instead of laces. This was an especially significant purchase since I arrived in Katowice wearing the same high lace-up shoes my father had given me before I left the ghetto. I had worn those shoes for four winters, and they were now tied to my feet with string. I was very happy to get rid of them, and I made a vow that one day I would have many shoes.

Aunt Sala proceeded to clean me up. She spent hours using a fine-tooth comb to clean my hair and remove the lice. The clothes I wore when I arrived in Katowice were burned in case there were still lice in them — washing alone did not seem to kill them. Of all the child-hood diseases I had and somehow recovered from without medical attention, the only thing that wouldn't go away was a nasty cough. Paulina had thought that I might have tuberculosis, but never took me to a doctor. One of the first things Auntie Sala did was take me to a doctor, where I received a proper diagnosis and antibiotics. Since Sala believed in home remedies, she also made me drink an awful concoction of hot milk with butter. I gagged on it the whole time it went down, but it cured the cough.

It took very little time to grow accustomed to the attention and affection everyone showered on me. I knew I was loved again. But as much as Aunt Sala embraced me, she wanted me to forget my Catholic past immediately. She told me, "You're Jewish, you're not Catholic. So get over it." I always knew I was Jewish, but after so many years of living as a Catholic, it was a central part of my life. After I left the Matusiewiczes I would often run to the nearest church. It felt safe and gave me solace. Sala would come in and drag me out. She could not bear the thought that I was a Catholic and could not easily change my beliefs. But I needed time to understand what had happened to me. How could I forget all those years overnight? Today I have a better understanding of what my aunt must have been going through. After losing her two children and entire family, she was afraid of losing me to the faith of my rescuers. But people didn't have a lot of psychological insight at this time, and she was suffering greatly. I told her that I would make a Catholic out of her before she made a Jew out of me. Had she let me be and let me leave Catholicism on my own terms, it would have been easier for both of us.

Fortunately, there were other surviving relatives who were more empathetic to my religious allegiance and sensitive about my significant transition from the Church back to Judaism. Zygmunt's brother, Stefan, and his second wife, Ania, lived in Lodz. They both had a terrible time during the war. Ania had survived on "Aryan" papers, moving from place to place, and had lost her entire family. Stefan was a printer who lived in the Przemyśl ghetto with his first wife. Located in the Krakow district, the ghetto had been divided into two parts: residential and a forced labour camp. German SS Sergeant Josef Schwammberger was the commander of various *Arbeitslager* (forced labour camps) and workshops in the district. On one occasion he sent Stefan by train, accompanied by two armed soldiers, to purchase or fix a printing press. Fearful that the soldiers were planning to kill him, Stefan slipped away and escaped from the train. When he made his way back to the ghetto, he learned that Schwammberger had had his wife killed as retribution for his actions.

Stefan fled the ghetto and spent the rest of the war on the run, hiding in barns and on farms. He was very ill for a long time after the war. Schwammberger was arrested for his crimes against humanity soon after liberation but escaped prosecution by fleeing to Argentina. After years of living under his own name (unlike most former Nazis, who assumed false identities to evade detection) in South America, the SS officer was tracked down and extradited to West Germany. Schwammberger was placed on trial, and Stefan was among those who testified against him. While never admitting his guilt, the Nazi was eventually found guilty of murder and accessory to murder in Przemyśl. Perhaps this verdict provided my dear cousin with a small measure of justice.

Stefan and Ania came to see me in Katowice and encouraged me to spend some time with them. I loved Stefan from the minute we met. He told me that he had lived in Lwów and was at the hospital with my parents when I was born. He knew my mother and father well and recalled how excited they were at my birth. Stefan told me that when they were about to perform the Caesarean, the doctor asked my father, "Who do you want to survive, your wife or your child?" My father replied, "I want them both."

Stefan was wonderful — patient and understanding. Even after going back to using my real name, Anita Helfgott, I was still afraid to be Jewish and was uneasy about everything. Stefan spent hours talking to me. He gently stressed that there was nothing to be afraid of any longer. I was safe with family, and the war was over. He talked to me about my family members who had been murdered: his four sisters and their families, his parents and his first wife. He wanted to take me to Lodz, where he and Ania had a lovely apartment, and I was eager to visit them. It was wonderful to be looked after and cared for by family. Since I had left my father, no one had hugged me or shown me love, and I was starved for it.

Stefan and Ania had a German Shepherd dog named Rex. He was twice my size and used to jump up on me to say hello. During my first visits to the apartment, he was territorial: as long I stayed on the floor, he was fine, but the minute I stepped onto the carpet he barked and charged at me. My experiences with animals were limited to the farm animals and that blasted cow at the parish, and I was petrified! After a while I stopped being afraid of him and we became friends. In Lodz, Ania took me to a library. I was so excited — I had never seen so many books in my life. I started to take out books, and I read and read. A few days after taking out books, I would return them and take more out. I fell in love with books.

While I was spending time with my cousins, Aunt Sala met and married a man named Danek. Nobody informed me of this marriage, and I could not decide what to make of it. I finally had my aunt, and here was another stranger. Before our reunion, Aunt Sala had acquired papers to leave Poland. The problem was that, besides my phony birth certificate, I had no identification papers. Somehow, Aunt Sala managed to attach a photo of me to her passport, claiming me as her daughter. We planned to travel to Paris, France, because my uncle Saul wrote that he would meet us there from the Belgian Congo. My cousin Stefan and his wife, Ania, also moved there. Aunt Sala's new husband, Danek, hoped to follow shortly after us.

My aunt tried to convince me that it would be exciting to see another country. Before leaving, we returned to Kluczbork to say goodbye to my rescuers. I had a short visit with them and with Father Michal's nieces, Ala and Basia. I did not realize how far Paris was and that this might be the last time we were together. I thought I could go back and forth any time to see them. Had I understood the true distance, I might have put up more of a fight. Instead, I was excited to be embarking on a new adventure during the summer break. And so, in August 1946, Sala and I left Poland.

The first stop on our train journey from Katowice was Warsaw. Warsaw had been bombed at the outbreak of war in 1939, and it experienced further destruction in the former Jewish quarter during the 1943 Warsaw Ghetto Uprising. In August 1944, Polish civilians revolted against the occupation in what later became known as the Warsaw Uprising. As punishment, Hitler ordered the city destroyed.

By the time we arrived in the summer of 1946, Warsaw was in ruins. I remember being very affected by the sight of all the rubble. Our next stop on the train was Prague. It was so soon after the war that the damage to Prague had not yet been repaired either, although it was not as bad as in Warsaw. I remember that one of the buildings in the main square was blackened by fire, and it seemed to me that the entire downtown sector was dug up.

From Prague we took a train and stopped in Munich for just one day. My aunt briefly entertained the idea of staying on in Germany, perhaps in one of the displaced persons camps, until I saw uniformed German soldiers — now prisoners — cleaning the rubble left by the Allied bombings. I couldn't bear the sound of their voices and became absolutely hysterical. It was far too soon to be in the company of our torturers. I gave my aunt a very hard time about not staying there and probably drove her crazy.

The next stop on our journey was Regensburg, Germany, so that Aunt Sala could pay a visit to the home of her rescuer, Oskar Schindler.

Sala thought quite fondly of the German and wanted to thank him for saving her life. Unfortunately, I was very unhappy with our outing. Wasn't it enough that I saw Germans on the street? Why did she have to take me to a German's house? At the time, I knew nothing of Schindler's wartime heroism except that he had rescued my aunt.

Schindler recognized my aunt immediately and invited us in. From what I can remember, he was a tall and strong-looking man, though he lacked the dashing good looks of the actor who later played him in the movie *Schindler's List*. He said hello to me, and that was the full extent of our conversation. His wife came out to say hello and serve us tea. Everyone spoke in German. I could not understand a word they said but remained on my best behaviour, thinking, "Why on earth did she have to bring me here?" The adults chatted for about an hour and then we left. I was very happy to get out of that home — I could not handle hearing German anymore. Perhaps I would have been happier at Schindler's home if my aunt had shared the reason for our visit. But she didn't, and the pair of us moved on to our final destination: Paris, France.

Sala and I arrived in Paris in the middle of August 1946. We proceeded to an address of some people my aunt knew from Sambor, a Mr. and Mrs. Koenig. Instead of taking a taxi, we hired a porter, who pushed our luggage through Paris while I sat on top of the suitcases. I can't imagine what people must have thought of us. It was ridiculous that my aunt did not order a taxi! The Koenigs took us in and fed us dinner. We were exhausted from our journey and quickly fell asleep. They were complete strangers to me, but kind. I do not recall seeing them again after our brief stay in their apartment, though perhaps my aunt maintained a friendship.

We did not want to impose on the Koenigs' generosity and decided to find a place of our own after a day or two. My aunt found a cheap hotel near the Arc de Triomphe, the Hotel Wagram. There were many other Holocaust survivors temporarily living in the hotel with us. My aunt befriended others like us, including a young Polish Jewish couple named Marian and Yetta Feldstein. They opened up quickly about their wartime trauma and their destroyed families. Yetta had golden hands. She was a talented knitter who could unravel a carpet and produce something magnificent. Her skill had helped her survive the war: she had moved from place to place, knitting to pay for her protection. Marian had been in the camps and was far more traumatized than his wife.

After a brief stay in Paris, the Feldsteins immigrated to New York as students, bypassing the Polish quota.[2] They eventually moved to Florida and opened a prosperous knitting factory. Our friendship

2   A US federal law, the Immigration Act of 1924, established immigration quotas based on nationality, limiting immigrants from each country to 2 per cent of that group's population in the United States. The law remained in effect until it was revised in 1952.

survived these life transitions, and I have fond memories of taking my children to visit their beautiful lake house. Yetta, who had been a closer personal friend to me, died years ago. Marian passed away more recently. I am happy to remain in touch with one of their sons, Simon.

When Aunt Sala wasn't busy working or socializing with her greenie friends, she worried about my preoccupation with Catholicism and my desire to locate churches in our new city. Auntie knew where I was the minute I disappeared. There was one church that I would go to for refuge; I even had "my" pew. It was a place that in a time of chaos and confusion meant comfort and security to me. I was understandably disillusioned after learning about my father's death and had ceased praying to Jesus for his return. But at the time, those unapproved church outings remained closely tied to Catholicism and the doctrine I had clung to throughout my time in hiding, even if I was no longer convinced that I believed. Auntie used to literally drag me out of church. She didn't understand that I was struggling to adjust to life in freedom, as a Jew. I couldn't just flip a switch and forget everything I had known.

Aunt Sala was determined to rectify my religious identity and signed me up for a Jewish camp in Switzerland through the Zionist youth movement Hashomer Hatzair. I could not yet speak French and didn't know a soul. We boarded a train and arrived in Switzerland a few hours later. On the way, the counsellors handed me a flag imprinted with the Star of David. All I could do was cry. The camp was in a beautiful setting, but I was so unhappy. Everything was just happening so quickly, and I could not stop crying. Soon, the counsellors put me on a train back to Paris. From the metro station I travelled to our hotel, convinced that my aunt would be very angry. However, she surprised me. Aunt Sala had missed me and was glad that I came back. She meant well when she sent me, but I was not ready to be sent to be with strangers again so soon. There had already been too much separation and too many changes in my short life. Besides that, Aunt Sala and I both needed each other desperately.

When we reunited, my aunt informed me that she had received a letter from Uncle Saul's wife, Elsa, in the Belgian Congo. Aunt Elsa wrote that Saul had died suddenly from a heart attack. I was terribly disappointed and upset that I would never meet him or his daughter, my cousin Irene. He had previously written to me that Irene was so happy to have a cousin and could not wait to meet me. Irene died of polio in 1950.

In the meantime, Sala and I could not continue to live in the hotel, as her husband, Danek, was expected to join us soon, so we went in search of a more permanent place to live. I don't know how my aunt knew where to look, but she found us a room near the Gare du Nord train station. The room had bare-bone furnishings: two beds, a table and chairs. There was a hotplate in one corner and a bathroom down the hall. My aunt bought a few things, and we settled in. Sometimes we spent time with Stefan and Ania, who lived nearby. Once a day, refugees would gather for a solid meal at the soup kitchen on Rue des Rosiers. These visits were traumatizing — I nearly had a fit every time we went. I didn't like the place and definitely did not want to be served meals there. I was very uncomfortable in the presence of so many Jews (Judaism was still an uneasy concept for me) and embarrassed to stand in line like cattle waiting to be fed. But I knew that I had no choice: even when she was working, my aunt was not making very much money, and she sought companionship from her contemporaries. In retrospect, I appreciate the French Jewish community for providing this service. Without these meals, many refugees might have gone hungry.

Shortly after we settled into our little room, Danek arrived in Paris. He stayed with us only a few days before taking off. I later realized that he had used Sala: he married her because she had papers allowing her to leave Poland, and marrying her would allow him to leave as well. Danek took advantage of her and hurt her badly. However, as I was still a child, my aunt told me very little about the situation. I understood not to raise questions and had no idea how or when she and Danek were divorced. All I knew was that he was out of our lives forever.

Since it was summer and there was no school, I stayed home alone once my aunt found a job in a factory where they were making children's coats from rabbit fur. One day while I was alone in our room, I began to have severe pain in my stomach. There was no way for me to get in touch with my aunt at her work. We had no phone and I did not know where she was working. By the time she came home I was really sick, vomiting and in terrible pain. She took me to the hospital, and I was diagnosed with appendicitis. The doctors performed surgery the same day, and I remained in the hospital for several more days. Since I did not speak French, I could not communicate with anyone until my aunt came to visit after work.

That fall I enrolled at the École de jeunes filles on Rue Milton. Since I'd only spent a brief time in school and had completely missed out on the building blocks and foundational skills of education, the administration placed me in a class with Grade 4 and 5 students, though at twelve years old, I should have been in Grade 6 or 7. Each morning I travelled a few metro stops by myself to get there. Our teacher was excellent, and I was excited to be back in school studying. I didn't speak a word of French when I arrived but learned the basics within a few months. Being surrounded by French speakers and being insecure in my inability to communicate sped up my learning process. My classmates were all very nice to me, but I formed no close friendships. I do not remember if any of the girls were Jewish because the subject never came up. What I do remember clearly was eating lunch in our classroom. The nine- and ten-year-olds used to bring sandwiches and wine. Who ever heard of kids drinking wine, let alone at school? But this was how things were done in Paris.

Even when I struggled, school was a joy. History was my favourite subject, but I found math exceedingly difficult, and I couldn't understand fractions for the life of me. Although I eventually got it, math was never my strong suit. Despite lagging behind in this area, I completed two grades in that first academic year and was awarded *le prix d'excellence* in recognition of my scholarly achievement. I was given a book with the award — Paul and Victor Margueritte's *Zette: histoire d'une petite fille* (Zette: The Story of a Little Girl), which remains in my possession to this day.

Around this time Hannah Edelman, who was originally from Sambor and knew my aunt Esther in New York, came to Paris to be with her husband, an officer with the American army who was stationed in Paris. Hannah was given our address in Paris and looked us up. Armed with parcels of clothing and toys from our American relatives, Hannah took me under her wing. Since there was no school on Thursdays, Hannah and I had a standing date every week, and we would travel all over the city together. She took me to eat at the American army restaurant and to visit French sites, including the Palace of Versailles. Hannah took me to see my first movie ever, *The Wizard of Oz*. It was beautiful. My American friend and I conversed in Polish, as she still remembered the language from her childhood in Sambor. We understood each other perfectly. Hannah made my life more interesting and less lonely when my aunt was at work. Her husband was discharged from his post after about a year, and they returned to New York. We remained in regular contact until the Edelmans passed away, many years later.

The summer of 1947 was a vast improvement over the previous one. My aunt arranged for the local Jewish community to pay for my room and board in the small village of Mont-Saint-Père. My hosts were a middle-aged Catholic couple, their son and an eighteen- or nineteen-year-old daughter named Solange. They were wonderful, caring people who showed a genuine interest in me. Solange took it upon herself to see that I enjoyed my time away from the city. I spent my days taking walks and playing outside with the local children.

My favourite memory of the summer was spending time in the river. Solange simply threw me in the water and told me to swim! I loved being with Solange, and in many ways this was my first taste of normal life. Unlike my teacher and classmates, Solange's family asked me many questions about my past: where I came from, who were my rescuers, what were my parents' fates. Interestingly, this was more than Canadians asked me for decades following my arrival in Canada. Perhaps the war was simply more present and real for French people, who had also suffered at the hands of the Nazis.

After that summer with Solange, I visited the library all the time. Since my favourite subject was history, I gravitated toward historical fiction. What I lacked in formal schooling I made up for as a quick thinker and skilled linguist. At the age of thirteen, I made huge strides and even read Victor Hugo's classic *Les Misérables* , an unusual choice for any young girl but especially a refugee whose mother tongue was not French. I took pride in my ability to read it in the original language. My advances did not go unnoticed by my teachers, and I received another scholarly award, *le prix d'honneur*, along with the book *Le Roman de Renart (Reynard the Fox)*. School was a very positive outlet for me.

The year after arriving in Paris, my aunt met Jack Goldstein, another survivor from Krakow. I was not happy to have someone else around, but I was a child and no one asked my opinion. Sala and Jack were married by a rabbi, a detail that I was informed of only after the ceremony. Jack simply showed up at our apartment with his bags, and my aunt told me, "This is your new uncle." All of a sudden, there was another new person in my life. I finally had my aunt all to myself and was disappointed by the disruption. It was very confusing to experience so many changes. But people in those days never told kids anything. There was a very different understanding of childhood and the impact such changes would have on a child's well-being. I knew better than to ask for any details about my aunt's life: if she wanted to share anything with me, she would.

Our growing family needed more room, and we moved to a small, two-room apartment at 26 Avenue d'Italie. The building had no elevator, and our fifth-floor unit was quite primitive. It had a tiny kitchen with a hot plate and two very small rooms to sleep in: one for my aunt and uncle and one for me. Our kitchen had a sink with cold running water. Toilets were communal and located between the floors, and since there was no seat we had to squat. We would heat water on the hot plate and wash up in the sink. Shower facilities were in a building with a *piscine*, swimming pool. The apartment was a tight squeeze, but this was typical for refugees. Now it was time for me to adapt to yet another life.

Sala's new husband, Jack Goldstein, was born in Krakow in 1908. He had owned and operated a pet shop before the war. When the Germans invaded, he and his first wife hoped to immigrate to Switzerland, but they were trapped like so many others. When the Goldsteins realized that deportation was imminent, they entrusted their two-year-old daughter, Tamara, to a former shop employee who was Catholic. Jack and his wife were deported to Auschwitz, where he was selected for labour in the Kanada barracks. His wife was murdered at Auschwitz.

Although Aunt Sala sometimes spoke about her Holocaust experiences with me, Uncle Jack shared nothing. Nearly all my knowledge about his three years in Auschwitz came from my aunt. Years later, I heard a story from a woman who had been with him in the Kanada barracks, where the inmates were forced to sort through the clothing that had been stolen from the Jews who had arrived on a recent transport. Many Jews had sewn diamonds and other jewels and money into their clothing when they realized they were going to be deported. "Organizing," or taking, these items — which would serve as valuable currency in the camp — was strictly forbidden, and any prisoner caught faced immediate death. As they worked, Jack could tell that this woman was tempted to slip an item into her pocket and warned her that the guards were watching closely. She told me that

my uncle had saved her life. Other details of his imprisonment are
scant.

Little, too, was known about Tamara's wartime experiences.
Renamed Helen Novak, she survived the war in hiding with her
Catholic rescuer. In 1946, the rescuer handed Tamara over to the
Jewish community in Krakow, and they placed her in an orphanage.
The entire orphanage was on its way to pre-state Israel when her father discovered that she was alive. After months of searching — and
after an illegal trip to Palestine — Jack eventually located the orphanage in Aix-les-Bains, a town in southeastern France. Tamara believed
she was an orphan and was shocked when a man showed up and
declared, "I am your father." She didn't know this man or have any
feelings toward him. She had been only two when they separated. Six
months later, he returned to the orphanage with Sala and told her,
"This is your mother." They refused to tell Tamara the truth, that her
mother had been murdered. What they did to me was equally cruel.
After hiding my Jewish identity for so long, I was forced to keep this
terrible secret as well. The secret was kept by me, my aunt and uncle
and presumably any surviving relatives. Out of respect for my aunt
and uncle, or perhaps out of concern for hurting Tamara, nobody
revealed the truth about her mother.

Well into adulthood, Tamara recalled nearly nothing about her
rescuers or her years in hiding. During a visit to Poland in 1989, I
asked the archivist at the Jewish Historical Institute in Warsaw to
search for anything related to Tamara Goldstein or Helen Novak
during the war. The search yielded no results. Then, in 2003, I received a call from the archivist: "Anita, you won't believe it, but I
found something on Tamara!" He asked if I could read Polish. I said
yes, and he faxed me the findings. The institute had recovered a de-
position about her rescuers. Through this mysterious document we
learned that the young female shop employee had turned the two-
year-old Jewish girl over to a Catholic aunt. The aunt claimed that

Helen Novak was her son's bastard child and hid the child for the entire war in an apartment. She was never allowed to go outside.

I remember my first meeting with Tamara well. My aunt and uncle had picked her up at the orphanage, and I was waiting anxiously to greet everyone at the metro station. I was wearing a coat with a rabbit-fur collar from my aunt's factory. The first thing seven-year-old Tamara said when she saw me was, "She has a collar! I want a collar!" She was jealous of my coat, but perhaps also the fact that I had been parented while she lingered in an orphanage for two years. Aunt Sala and Jack insisted that we share my small bed and we slept head-to-feet. While I didn't complain, Tamara made up for the two of us, whining about having to sleep beside me. We were complete strangers to each other, and she was uncomfortable. I was too, but over the years I had learned not to express feelings of discontent.

Sixty years later, Tamara recalled these same events, noting that she had no contact with other children until the age of five, and then, as the youngest child in the orphanage, she had little to do with the other children there. She remembers that she was jealous of me, not wanting to share her newly found father and mother. Soon, however, she saw me as someone who could introduce her to the wider world. Not long after we met, for example, I took her to the opera. I collected some small change, and we paid for standing room behind a pillar, right under the roof.

Since my aunt and uncle worked, I assumed responsibility for escorting Tamara to and from school. Each morning we left the apartment and walked to the metro station. As a result of her years in hiding, Tamara was a tiny girl and physically frail. When we would go down the stairs to the subway, she would sit on the stairs and not move. I didn't know what was wrong with her. Maybe her muscles were weak? Was she tired? What was I supposed to do? I could not pick her up and carry her. So we would simply wait until she decided to continue down the stairs, which led to many late arrivals at school.

I was six years older than Tamara and knew that the changes were also difficult for her. She had been told that she was an orphan and then, suddenly, had parents and an adopted sister. It was difficult for Tamara to join a family in all that confusion, and it took time for her to make sense of it all. I could certainly sympathize. Unfortunately, I was too young and ignorant of psychology at the time to support her. As an adult, Tamara is still physically frail but has emotional strength and intelligence. I am very proud of her for overcoming so much and building a rich and meaningful life for herself.

While Tamara was adjusting to family life after being in an orphanage, I was free to roam Paris alone and grew to know the city well. When Princess Elizabeth and Prince Philip came to Paris in May 1948, I ran around the city like a crazy person so that I could see the princess at every stop on her itinerary. It was an exciting time for me. Little by little I also began to reclaim my Jewish identity. Auntie Sala slowly reintroduced a few Jewish traditions into our home life. Even though she was not observant, we occasionally attended synagogue with Uncle Jack. And as with Christmas Mass in Rozdół, I did not know what was happening during the services. I never studied Hebrew and couldn't read the prayers. Fortunately, my French was strong enough that I could understand the French translation in the prayer book. I realized that all the people I met at the synagogue and in our community were Jewish and that they were good people. As I heard their stories of what they had lived through, I came to realize that I needed to be proud of my origins and remain Jewish for my parents' sake. Gradually, I stopped going to church. I do not recall experiencing any antisemitism during that time. Auntie Sala and Uncle Jack got along well then, and our home was quiet and peaceful.

The declaration of Israel as a state in May 1948 was a momentous occasion in Paris and helped me reaffirm pride in my Jewishness. Aunt Sala and Uncle Jack took Tamara and me to an outdoor event in Paris' Jewish quarter. The refugees gathered in the street for a celebration. Like my family, many of the refugees were still in transit, waiting to move on to their final destinations. The survivors, who were mostly adults, danced in the street, proudly singing the unofficial Israeli national anthem, Hatikvah. But despite this historic moment, they could not truly celebrate after everything they had experienced. Instead, everybody cried tears of joy mixed with bitterness. Why couldn't this have happened ten years earlier?

I was thirteen years old at the time and did not fully comprehend what was going on. Months earlier we had sat at home around our little portable radio as the United Nations votes that would determine the future of Palestine were counted. We had all listened intently for the results, crossing our fingers that the November 1947 resolution enabling Israel to declare statehood would pass. I could not quite grasp that the Jews had no state before this. My aunt pointed out to me that it was too late for our dead. When the Nazis set their sights on Europe's Jews, no country wanted to open its doors for us. Perhaps if Israel had existed then, Jews might have had a safe haven to turn to, and the Holocaust would never have happened.

# No Longer a Refugee

My aunt applied for us to immigrate to the United States, home to her sister Esther and her brother Elias Gottlieb, their spouses and my cousins. Unfortunately, we were classified as Poles and subject to the Polish quota, which was still in existence. The list of Poles waiting to immigrate to the United States was very long, and we would have had to wait years in France before we could leave. In early 1948, my aunt heard that Canada would be allowing Jews to enter through close relative sponsorships. In 1939, this opportunity had been out of the question: a government bureaucrat offered the line that "none is too many," in response to the question of how many Jewish refugees Canada should grant entry to. This happened at a time of a highly stringent and discriminatory immigration policy overseen by Frederick Charles Blair, a noted antisemite. But by 1948, Canada's doors had slowly widened to accept European Jews seeking new homes. My aunt Esther had a friend from her hometown of Sambor whose brother, Sidney Zeiler, was living in Toronto. My relatives approached Sidney, and he generously agreed to prepare the necessary paperwork to bring Sala and me to Canada.

One day, after a long wait, my aunt came home and announced that our visas had arrived — we were moving to Canada, though Uncle Jack and Tamara had to remain in Paris until my aunt could sponsor them. Nobody discussed any of these decisions with me.

I would have been happy to stay in Paris. I loved going to school, and I loved the hustle and bustle of the city. But did I have any say in the matter? Absolutely not. Nobody asked my opinion. I don't think Aunt Sala asked Jack's opinion either. He had two brothers who had survived the war and settled in Australia and Israel, but going to either of those places was never discussed. My aunt had a very strong personality, and she was the one who made decisions about the family's future. She was determined to reunite with her relatives in New York, and so this was the only viable option. At the same time, I was excited to meet my mother's family. They had sent us care parcels with clothing and toys and warm letters expressing how much they wanted us to immigrate.

Several months earlier, our cousins Stefan and Ania had obtained immigration visas to Venezuela. Everyone was trying to get out of post-war Europe, and they took the first opportunity presented to them. Stefan's brother, Zygmunt, a professor at the University of Warsaw, and his family stayed in Poland. When it became increasingly difficult for Jews to stay in Poland because of persecution, Stefan brought Zygmunt and his wife, Lucia, and his two daughters, Bogusia and Ania, to Venezuela, in 1957. The brothers eventually established prosperous careers, Zygmunt as a professor of engineering at the Central University of Venezuela and Stefan as the owner of a successful luggage factory. I maintained a close relationship with Stefan and Ania, as well as with their son Luis. I travelled to Venezuela several times to visit them, the last time shortly before Stefan's death.

As our departure grew closer, I became increasingly excited. When I think back to that time now, I imagine that it must have been very difficult for Aunt Sala to leave her husband and stepdaughter behind. But we had a chance to get out and could not pass that up. There was very little to do in preparation for our move. When we fled Poland, Auntie's papers stated that I was her daughter. For this trip, I acquired a stateless passport in Paris and would travel to Canada on my own passport with my real name. My parents' names were also listed, although my mother's name was written incorrectly as Elsa Helfgott. Her family referred to her as Ettela, and her Polish name was Edzia. Somebody likely filled in the paperwork incorrectly. Neither Aunt Sala nor I raised this error with immigration. Who knows how they might have responded? And with that, the next leg of my journey began.

In August 1948, Auntie Sala and I began preparations for our journey across the Atlantic. We packed a single suitcase apiece. My luggage included a few pieces of clothing and the two books I had won at school. Auntie packed some personal belongings and a goose-feather comforter. I have no idea why. What I do recollect is that when my aunt Esther saw it upon our arrival in Toronto, she begged her sister to give it to her. I guess she hadn't seen something like it in God knows how long. But Auntie Sala refused to part with the comforter. After all, we had so little to begin with. In terms of money, we had peanuts! Maybe twenty dollars to our name.

Once our bags were packed and documents ready, Auntie and I took a train to Nice. Uncle Jack and Tamara did not join us for this leg of the trip. We said our goodbyes in Paris, hoping that they would be able to follow us to Toronto in short order. From Nice we moved on to Cannes, a beautiful resort town in the French Riviera. We spent a bit of time there basking in the perfect weather. When it was time to leave, porters directed all passengers into little boats that took us to the ship. I was so excited for this adventure to begin!

We sailed from Cannes on the SS *Sobieski*, a Polish ship named in honour of a seventeenth-century Polish king. It was a very large vessel that had been converted for wartime use and then returned to civilian service in 1947. Everything about it was marvellous. As tourist-class travellers, our windowless berth was in the hold, the ship's lowest level. We shared our room, which was outfitted with two sets of bunk beds, with two strangers.

If the sleeping conditions were poor, they didn't faze me one bit. In fact, I barely spent any time in our berth and avoided it as much as possible. It was August, and I was outside the entire time, enjoying the journey on the main deck and in the on-board swimming pool. Sometimes there was even a movie screening. The ship was swarming with people — I loved it. At one point the ship stopped in Gibraltar, and we were surrounded by lots of little fishing boats selling souvenirs and other items. But even if I had wanted to buy anything, I didn't have any money.

Fortunately, I wasn't stricken with any sea sickness while we were on calm seas. My poor aunt, on the other hand, was sick the whole trip! She spent the entire time throwing up in a bathroom in the hold and would eat oranges in an effort to manage her nausea. I would bring them to her from the dining room and run out of the berth as fast as I could. I'd never seen an orange before and wondered what it was. I personally found them too sour, but I guess they helped her.

Most of my memories of the trip are wrapped up in one boy. At the beginning of the trip I met a group of American teenagers returning from their French vacations. Among them was a young man who caught my attention. I will never forget the name of my first crush: George Demetriu. He was about sixteen and very cute; I was fourteen and enamoured. I believe his family was Greek-American and lived in a fancy part of New York State. Apparently, they were quite well-to-do, so his room was located on a more desirable level of the ship. George had spent the previous year studying in France and was returning to New York for the next school year. He and his older sister were travelling together. She was about eighteen years old and probably starting university that September. I recall that she was very nice and very beautiful, and that all the men on the ship were interested in her. George and I communicated in French and spent much of the trip swimming, talking and watching movies. It was wonderful.

When the ship docked in New York City, George and I said our goodbyes, exchanged addresses and pledged to stay in touch. But it was not to be. George never wrote to me, so I didn't write him. All I know is that he made the trip a great deal of fun for me.

On August 15, 1948, the SS *Sobieski* docked at Pier 21 in Halifax, Nova Scotia. With our luggage in tow, Auntie Sala and I had to go through Canadian immigration. There were hordes of tourist-class passengers waiting in line to be processed, one at a time. Our immigration officer asked us what seemed like a million questions and scrutinized our papers. I imagine someone spoke to us in French, as we didn't know any English, but I cannot recall for certain. After what seemed like an eternity, the officer stamped my French travel visa with the words "landed immigrant." That was golden in those days. I, Anita Helfgott, was no longer a refugee. It was a proud moment.

After finally being processed, somebody directed us to the train station in Halifax, where we boarded a train headed to Toronto. It was a long trip, and we stopped overnight in Montreal. I couldn't figure out where I was. Although I was completely fluent in French, I could not understand a word the Québécois spoke. It was not Parisian French! Auntie Sala knew only a few words of French. She had not attended language classes in Paris, and all of her colleagues and friends there had been Jewish refugees who spoke Yiddish amongst themselves. But she got by without a problem, and I stepped up as translator when necessary.

A crowd greeted us at Union Station in Toronto. My Auntie Esther Begleiter was there with her daughter Sylvia, Sylvia's husband, Ted Korotkin, and their eleven-year-old son, Michael. Esther had three daughters, but Sylvia and Ted were very well off and were the only ones who had the means to come to Toronto to meet us. Somehow Ted managed to get onto the platform and was running along the train calling, "Stern, Stern" — my aunt Sala's name from her first marriage to Victor Stern. I asked Auntie Sala not to answer because I was scared: for all I knew, it could be some Jewish committee trying to take me away. It was silly, but I was afraid of everything. Of course, she replied that everything was fine and that she was expecting Ted. Nobody would ever take me away again.

As Ted accompanied us from the platform to the station, the tears started flowing. It was an emotional reunion between the sisters. They cried and cried and cried. It was my first time meeting Aunt Esther and the cousins. I believe they were happy to see me. Auntie Sala had written to them from Paris, so they already knew how I'd survived the Holocaust. It was a relief to not have to talk to them about it and relive such painful memories so soon after my arrival. Ted brought the car around and then drove us straight to the home of Jean and Sidney Zeiler. One thing that stood out for me on the drive was the sign atop the Royal York Hotel. It was so flashy and kept blinking; it definitely grabbed my attention.

The Zeilers lived on Glenholme Avenue near Vaughan Road and St. Clair Avenue. They welcomed us with open arms, just like we were family. They had a five-year-old son, Johnny, and a one-year-old daughter, Cheryl. Aunt Sala and I had dinner, took a bath and went straight to bed. Auntie and the others communicated in Yiddish, which I could not understand, and Johnny followed us around, asking his mother, "Why can't these people talk?" My aunt and I slept a great deal during our first days in Toronto. It had been an exhausting trip for Auntie Sala because she had been so ill, and for me because of all the socializing and the sheer excitement of the adventure.

My American relatives had rented rooms at the Park Plaza Hotel at Avenue Road and Bloor Street and stayed in Toronto for a few nights as we settled in. They visited us at the Zeilers and took us out for a few meals before returning to New York. During this visit, my cousin Michael Korotkin and I developed a strong connection, and we have enjoyed a warm relationship since that first meeting.

After a few days at the Zeilers, it was time to find our own place to live. Jean helped us find a room a few blocks away on Cherrywood Avenue in the home of Sia Silverman and her husband (whose name I cannot recall). It was a house with a wide porch, and Auntie and I had a room upstairs with a bed, a little table, chairs and a hot plate. The house was well maintained and Sia was kind and helpful. She had a sweet little girl named Loretta, with whom I spent lots of time.

Aunt Sala began work almost immediately. Her first job was stitching piecework at Paradise Dress & Waist on Spadina Avenue. Sidney Zeiler's clothing factory was nearby, and Auntie Sala travelled to work with him until she felt comfortable taking the streetcar on her own. I imagine that Sidney helped her find the job: how could she have found it on her own? It is also conceivable that she received job advice and financial assistance through the Jewish Immigrant Aid Society (JIAS), though I never visited the offices with her. My aunt worked exceptionally hard to care for me and build a new life for us. As soon as we arrived in Canada, Aunt Sala started going by the anglicized "Sally," and this is what I called her for the rest of her life.

A couple of weeks after we landed, the school year began. After taking Johnny to his first day of kindergarten, Jean Zeiler registered me for classes at Humewood Public School. Auntie couldn't register me herself: she could not speak English and was busy at work. I was fourteen years old, and they put me in Miss Phillips's Grade 8 class. I believe I was slightly older than the others. Until beginning at Humewood, I had fewer than three years of formal education: a few months in Poland after the war and two years in France. I had to learn English and was behind in math. Miss Phillips spent a lot of time with me. She was a dedicated educator and knew that I was an orphan from Poland. I don't know if she knew about my wartime experiences or how I lost my parents. Decades later, once I was married with children, I attended a school reunion; I recognized Miss Phillips immediately, and she was still lovely and kind. I was so pleased when she remembered me.

Some of my Humewood classmates were Jewish, and everyone was welcoming to me. A few of them tried to help me improve my English during breaks. Every day at lunchtime I came home to make myself something to eat. The foods that surprised me most were peanut butter and cereal; they were so different from French cuisine! While these foods were novelties to me, I was a novelty at school. Once I could communicate in English, my peers asked me many questions:

Where was I born? Where did my family come from? Where had I immigrated to Canada from? Stuff like that. Most did not ask about my survival of the Holocaust, and to those that did ask, I replied that I was an orphan and came from Paris. Although some of my peers were curious, I was always careful not to volunteer too much information, and, in any event, I wasn't yet confident enough to respond to a lot of personal questions in English. It took a long time for me to trust others with my history. By the time I entered high school, my peers' curiosity diminished. It might not have occurred to Canadian teenagers, separated from the events of the Holocaust by distance and experience, to ask about my experiences during the war. Maybe it was too foreign or they were afraid their questions would upset me, or maybe their parents warned them to avoid intrusive personal questions. In any case, I wanted to be like all the other teenagers and fit in. I did not want to talk about the war, even with my closest girlfriends.

Throughout that first year in Toronto, attaining fluency in English was my top priority. I quickly learned the alphabet but possessed no vocabulary and could not pronounce or understand the words I was reading. Twice a week I attended special night-school classes offered by JIAS for Holocaust survivors. On alternate evenings, female volunteers from the Canadian Jewish Congress and JIAS helped me to improve my language skills at their homes. While I loved learning, that first year was a struggle, and my first semester at Humewood was disastrous! I performed slightly better in the second semester and by the third, I received good marks. I worked very hard and could speak English by the end of the first school year. However, I still had to write every single entrance exam in order to advance to high school at Vaughan Road Collegiate. My distinctive accent — Polish mixed with Parisian French — never bothered me. Similarly, I never paid much attention to my aunt and uncle's accents.

Although I was friendly with my classmates and a girl from my neighbourhood, I rarely socialized outside of school because I was so busy studying. Auntie Sally, on the other hand, made a whole bunch of greenie friends very quickly. Many other survivor women were also working in factories and workshops on Spadina Avenue. My future mother-in-law was part of that community and did piecework at the Tip Top Tailors factory. These women made their own little community and supported one another. My aunt was very happy during this time.

Since Auntie worked very long days, I spent hours after school with Sia doing my homework and practising English. I also played with her daughter Loretta, a real sweetie. The Zeilers were very good to us and sometimes invited us for Shabbat dinner. As soon as I learned enough English, I spent much of my free time babysitting for Loretta, Johnny and Cheryl. With the pocket change I earned, I bought myself books, the first and most treasured of them being *Little Women*. In the evenings, my aunt would prepare dinner for the two of us on our hot plate. We didn't have fancy meals, just a piece of fish or something small. But she always made sure we ate. We rarely had dinner in the dining room with our landlords.

Uncle Jack and Tamara planned to come to Toronto in mid-1949, about nine months after Auntie and I arrived. The four of us could not all live in one room, so we moved to 749½ Queen Street West just after I completed Grade 8. Auntie and I prepared the place before they arrived. The apartment was located above a wallpaper store owned by a Jewish man named Weiser. There were lots of mice in that building. One day my friend Helen and I were in the kitchen and heard some scratching in a drawer. I opened the drawer and saw a mouse, pulled the drawer out and took it outside while Helen stood on a chair screaming.

Aunt Sally and Uncle Jack were remarried at City Hall in Toronto. Tamara and I were not told when or where the ceremony would take place. Tamara, of course, thought that they were both her biological parents. We began to live together as a family in the Queen Street apartment. It had three rooms: there was a kitchen at the back of the store and two rooms and a bathroom upstairs. Aunt Sally and Uncle

Jack shared one bedroom; Tamara and I shared the other, as well as the single bed where we again slept head to toe. It was not comfortable in the least. The bigger challenge than our cramped space was Tamara's behaviour. She was a real brat! I had to take care of her after school, but she never listened to me. She refused to speak French with me and made fun of my fading French accent.

There's one early memory that particularly stands out. Tamara and I were home alone and I needed to bathe her, and Tamara resisted with all her strength. She wouldn't listen to me and refused to get in the bathtub. So, I shoved her in. Tamara yelled and screamed so loudly that I'm sure the whole street could hear. When my aunt came home from work, Mr. Weiser stopped her and said, "You had better go straight upstairs. One of the girls might be dead." Needless to say, I enjoyed the time we spent apart.

Although we were not highly observant, Judaism had a presence in our home. Auntie Sally prepared delicious Shabbat dinners and Passover seders for our little family, even when finances were tight. We did not belong to a synagogue in those days. Who could afford it? Somehow, Auntie always ensured we had tickets to Rosh Hashanah and Yom Kippur services. She was very resourceful and intelligent. Thanks to her intervention, during the summer after Grade 8, the local Jewish Camp Fund sent me to the girls-only Camp B'nai Brith on Lake Couchiching. Oh, how I loved that camp! It was a wonderful three-week respite from life in the city and from pesky Tamara. Everybody at the camp was my own age — no little kids in sight. My favourite activity was swimming in the lake, and I particularly liked one of the swim counsellors. To the best of my knowledge, I was the only Holocaust survivor in my bunk. All the other campers were Canadian-born. We became quick friends, and nobody questioned my accented-yet-fluent English. I did not want to return home when the camp session came to an end.

The move to Queen Street West occurred the summer before I entered high school, and since our school district had changed, I could not go to high school where I wrote my entrance exams. Instead, I enrolled for classes at the Central High School of Commerce. A funny story: In those days, students who did not live with their parents had to register with the Board of Education. Aunt Sally couldn't miss work to accompany me — every penny counted. I signed some piece of paper and showed the Board of Education officials my stateless passport. At the office there was another girl, Vera, who lived with her sister Ricky. The two of us just looked at each other and didn't say a word. When school started a few days later, we bumped into each other in class. One of us asked the other, "Didn't I see you last week at the Board of Education?" Vera and I have been good friends from that moment on.

The first day of Grade 9 was great. I already spoke English fluently so there were no communication problems. We received our timetables and quite a few books. Because nobody could afford to buy them, the school loaned us the books for free. In addition to meeting Vera, I was introduced to four other amazing Jewish girls: Helen, Sheila, Marlene and Golda. We are all still friends today, though Sheila unfortunately died a few years ago. These girls accepted me as a regular teenager, and I felt like a normal girl around them. We all joined a group at the B'nai Brith house on the northwest corner of Spadina Avenue and College Street, right next door to a funeral parlour. Our B'nai Brith counsellor came up with all kinds of fun programming ideas. We attended dances with the boys' groups, enjoyed outings around the city and had group meetings. This was a great way to meet new people. Sometimes we volunteered at the seniors' home. We served the residents tea, spoke with them and put on some performances. We had great fun together.

My first year at Central Commerce was successful. I did well in my classes and learned penmanship, typing, shorthand and some bookkeeping. On school holidays, we girls would walk along College Street, which was then at the hub of Jewish life in Toronto — the place to see and be seen. When we had a little bit of money, we would drop into Becker's and buy hot dogs. What a treat! While I enjoyed close friendships and school, Toronto could never compete with Paris from a cultural and lifestyle standpoint. Toronto had all these blue laws: on Sundays you couldn't go to a movie, and shops were closed. I remember only half-jokingly kvetching to Aunt Sally, "Why did you bring us here? You couldn't have found somewhere else?" It was Toronto the terrible to me. The city has improved dramatically over the years but still cannot compare to Paris. While living on Queen Street, I worked in a grocery store after school and on weekends. I bought a used bicycle with my first ten dollars, and once I had wheels, I rode it all over and loved it.

At the end of my first high school year, I visited New York for the first time. My cousins Renee and Pearl shared a rental cottage in the Catskills. I was nearly sixteen, and they invited me to spend the entire summer with them. It was exciting to spend so much time surrounded by family. My cousins were in their thirties and were married with children. Both of their husbands had served in the American army during the war. There were a bunch of young people working as counsellors at the local Jewish camp, and I became friends with them for that summer. Renee and Pearl even threw me a surprise party for my sweet sixteen. That day, somebody took me for a drive into the country, and when we returned...surprise! Happy birthday to me! They invited all of my counsellor friends to the celebration. It was a wonderful, wonderful visit.

Following my stay in the Catskills, I went to New York to visit my other relatives. Uncle Eli and his wife, Dorothy, hosted me first. Their two sons were both in graduate school, Stanley for law and Shelley for physiology. The three of us were fairly close in age and spent a lot of time together. More notably, I ate very well, as Aunt Dorothy was an excellent cook. I particularly loved her chocolate pudding, and she made it for me daily and let me lick the pot. From there I stayed with my aunt Esther, whose husband, Iser, had recently died. When I asked, Esther would answer questions about my mother. The trouble was that my mother was a young woman when Esther emigrated, so she could tell me only about my mother's training at the commercial school and about her office work. Esther spoke of my mother's good looks, but I remembered that from when I was a little girl. Unfortunately, Esther did not know my father at all because she was already in New York when my parents built their life together. I couldn't ask Aunt Sally these questions about my parents because she would start crying. I never wanted to upset her and learned to remember my former life in silence.

Although I had an excellent summer, I was eager to return to school and my friends. At the time, our family was renting a flat, one floor of a house at 9 Roblock Avenue. My friend Sheila lived very close by, and I visited her home often. Every time her father spotted me walking up the street, he would sing out, "The shrimpboat is coming!" He loved poking fun at the pair of us because I was so little and Sheila was so tall. His singing always made me laugh. I imagined that this was how my father would have been.

Grade 10 was another good year. My only problem at school was that I couldn't see the chalkboard. I complained to my aunt, but she didn't believe that I had a vision problem; she thought I was faking it because I wanted glasses like my friend Helen. Helen and I came up with a solution. She sat behind me and we passed her glasses back and forth, taking turns reading from the board. This went on for months before I finally convinced my aunt that I was going to be in big trouble at school if I didn't get my eyes checked. Turns out, I was nearly blind, and I've worn glasses until I had cataract surgery a few years ago. The same thing happened to Tamara a few years later, except I believed her right away and, with my meagre earnings, bought her the glasses that our parents had refused to get her. This caused a fight with Aunt Sala, who threw the glasses across the room, saying that I was meddling.

From the moment I started school, my hope was to graduate high school and continue on to university. After all, I was a high achiever and loved learning, and I wanted to be a teacher. My aunt loved me very much but did not support my academic ambitions. She wanted me to find a job to help support the family instead of focusing all my attention on my education and girlfriends. For two years I attended school during the day and worked evenings and Saturdays at the Brighton Laundry. My job was to stand at one end of a huge roller, opposite another employee at the other end, and catch and fold the sheets as they came off. It was very difficult work because I was small. I handed most of my earnings over to my aunt, holding onto a small amount for social outings.

At the end of the summer after Grade 10, any plans for higher education were placed on hold indefinitely. Aunt Sally told me that my salary was vital to the family. Her own job paid insufficiently, and Uncle Jack found it difficult to maintain employment. In order to stay afloat, they needed me to contribute to the household income. I was very unhappy to leave Central Commerce and my friends but had no choice. I secured a secretarial job in the order department at Tip Top Tailors on Front Street. My boss was a decent man named Mr. Woodbridge. I worked from 9:00 a.m. to 5:00 p.m., and it took me one hour to get there and back by bus and then streetcar. My days were filled with typing up and filing purchase invoices. My starting salary was twenty-two dollars a week, fifteen of which I gave to Auntie for room and board. The situation was not ideal, but that's just the way it was.

# The Love of My Life

Our family still lived at 9 Roblock Avenue when I met the love of my life, Frank Ekstein. The introduction came about in a strange manner. Frank had a childhood friend named Gerry Cohen. Gerry's parents were from Czechoslovakia and were friends with Frank's parents. Gerry knew a girl named Thelma Ambrose, who I knew through my B'nai Brith group. Why Thelma passed along my phone number to Gerry, I'll never know. I had not seen Thelma for quite some time and I did not know Gerry and Frank did not know Thelma. Perhaps Thelma told Gerry that I was from Poland, and Gerry thought Frank might like to meet me. In any case, Frank called to ask me out. As they say, it was *bashert* (meant to be).

I remember that first telephone conversation with Frank when I told him I wasn't interested. I was reluctant to accept his offer immediately because of an earlier incident. Auntie Sally had fixed me up on a blind date with a man named Herbie who lived in Leamington, Ontario. Herbie's parents were from Sambor, and Aunt Sally wanted me to make a good impression on Herbie. The date was a disaster. I did not like him and refused to go out with him again. My aunt was disappointed; she had hoped something might come of our match. His parents were well off, and his mother was a landsman, from the same part of Europe as us, and my aunt would have considered it a perfect match.

Frank was very persistent. Despite being a shy man (as I learned later), he called me three times to ask me out. I eventually agreed on the condition that we each brought along a friend, as I would be more comfortable with that arrangement. Frank agreed and we arranged to meet on December 21, 1951. I had invited my good friend Marlene, and Frank brought his friend Fritzie. Frank also arranged for his friends Erica (Fritzie's sister), Ernie Bloch, Harry Gould and Eva Fantl to join us. Erica, Fritzie, Harry and Ernie were all Holocaust survivors, and Eva's parents were also from Czechoslovakia. None of the couples were married at the time. Many years later, Ernie participated on the March of the Living with me, and we spent a lot of time reminiscing about the past. Unfortunately, Ernie died the following year.

I remember being very nervous before the date. Our landlady, Rusia, opened the door for Frank and called to me to come downstairs. As I came down the stairs, I glanced at the door to see what this person looked like — he was good-looking. Frank looked me over and said hello. We met Fritzie outside and went to pick up Marlene. We all met at the Uptown Theatre on Yonge Street. Frank's friends were waiting in the lobby. I was introduced to everyone and was told that Ernie, Erica and Harry had come to Canada after the war.

During the movie Frank asked me to go out with him on New Year's Eve. I said that I would think about it. I later learned that the following day Frank went to Hamilton and told his cousins Richard and Joe Popper that he had met the girl he was going to marry! Actually, I felt the same way, but it would take another three and a half years before it would happen.

After the movie, we went to Tops Restaurant at Yonge and Bloor Streets, around the corner from the theatre. Unbeknownst to me, Ernie had had an unsettling encounter with an usher before we left the theatre. And wouldn't you know it, the usher followed us to our nightcap. Ernie went outside to settle the matter and then returned to the diner and informed us that the usher would not be bothering us anymore. I had no idea what happened, but Ernie later revealed that the usher made some disparaging remarks about Jews. Ernie was a tough guy, and I am sure he gave the usher a hard time. Every time I saw Ernie after this night, I remembered him defending us.

Frank and I spoke several times on the phone and shared our histories. Frank told me that he was born in a suburb of Prague and that he was six years old when his family fled to Canada in May 1939 on one of the last boats carrying Czech Jewish passengers; they were permitted to enter Canada as farmers. Thanks to the foresight of a relative named Karl Abeles, numerous members of Frank's extended family survived the Holocaust. As Hitler started expanding his power, Karl recognized that Europe was no longer safe for Jews, and he became determined to get his loved ones out. Karl immigrated to Canada first to assess the situation and report back to the rest of the family. Between November 1938 and the summer of 1939, Karl helped orchestrate his extended family's escape to Canada as refugee farmers despite Canada's infamous and discriminatory "none is too many" policy concerning the immigration of Jewish refugees.

I told Frank that I was born in Poland and came to Canada after the war. I did not share details about my wartime survival with him until much later. I was seventeen and Frank had just turned nineteen on December 12, nine days before we met. I was going to night school, and Frank was already working for Falcon Lumber and attending Shaw Business College at night. He had graduated from Harbord Collegiate the previous June. We were just young kids, and yet there was something there between us.

I had already been invited to the New Year's Eve party that Frank invited me to, and I already had a date. I did an awful thing. There was such an immediate connection and attraction to Frank that I broke my original date and went with Frank instead. From then on, Frank and I were together all the time.

Neither of us owned a car, so Frank would come to pick me up on the streetcar. Ernie had a van and we all used to go out together to movies and dances. One night, a group of us went out to see a movie and were travelling home in the van. At the time, Frank was a smoker, and he put a used cigarette in the pocket of his new coat. He didn't know the fire wasn't out until suddenly, the car stank of smoke. Frank had burned a hole straight through the pocket of his new coat. He knew that his parents had worked hard to buy the coat and felt guilty that he ruined it. So he got his uncle Willy (his father's younger brother) to pay for the coat to be invisibly mended without his parents' knowledge. And they never found out.

Several weeks after our first date, Frank took me to meet his relatives in Hamilton. One of his father's sisters, Aunt Heda, her husband, Uncle Alois Popper, and his cousins Richard (Dick) and Joe lived on a dairy farm in Mount Hope, near Hamilton. They were the last of the 1939 arrivals to remain farmers. During the same visit, I met another one of Frank's aunts, Aunt Ida, who lived with her husband, Uncle Leo Abeles near the farm. Their two daughters, Hannah and Mina, were already married and raising families of their own.

Frank's father, Ernest, was a cattle dealer and had qualified for a permit to immigrate with his wife, Anna, and two sons, Frank and Paul. He then successfully secured visas for his wife's sisters and brothers, their spouses and her elderly mother. Unfortunately, Ernest's two sisters refused to leave because they could not bring their furniture with them. They remained behind in Czechoslovakia and did not survive. The Eksteins' story was later featured in Irving Abella and Harold Troper's book, *None Is Too Many: Canada and the Jews of Europe 1933–1948*.

The Eksteins landed on Ontario farms: they had abandoned their wealth and material possessions, lands and homes, culture and lifestyle, and left behind those loved ones who could not make the journey. But they were alive. Everyone initially settled on farms in Southern Ontario to complete a three-year farming contract with the Baron de Hirsch farming project, which created agricultural colonies for Jewish immigrants from Eastern Europe. The family was extremely close, and Frank was best friends with his first cousins Dick and Joe. Over the years we spent a lot of time on the family farm. I met Dick Popper's wife, Doris, who later told me that everyone in the family knew that I was a Holocaust survivor, but they never talked about it or asked questions because they were afraid it would be too painful for me to discuss. This was the case with all of my girlfriends — we just didn't talk about it.

Frank's immediate family had relocated to Toronto after the war. His younger brother by two years, Paul, was attending university in Guelph at the time. I did not meet any of them until we were serious about each other. Frank introduced me to his parents, Ernest and Anna, several months after we began dating. Anna had attended finishing school in Switzerland, and Ernest had been a well-to-do landowner with a car and chauffeur. Their backgrounds were very different from mine.

Frank and Paul had absolutely no Jewish education, and the family was so assimilated that Frank only received his Hebrew name, Zev, before our wedding because his parents could not remember his original Hebrew name. The Eksteins ate different food than I was used to, moved in different circles and had different experiences than my Polish relatives did. Ernest thought that Frank was too young to be in such a serious relationship and had no business dating just one girl. There was a rumour that my future father-in-law didn't want his elder son to marry a Polish girl, implying that I was not good enough for their family. Needless to say, they placed numerous obstacles in our way. My aunt Sally, on the other hand, thought we should get married immediately. "What are you schlepping around for?" she, and others, asked, wondering what the delay was. It was the 1950s and unusual for couples to date for extended periods of time before deciding to get married.

Other friends of ours were quicker to tie the knot. In 1952, Frank and I were guests at two weddings: those of Ernie and Erica, and Harry and Eva. They were beautiful events. We knew that our relationship was also headed toward marriage, but we were in no rush. Frank introduced me to his best friend, Henry Seldon, whom he had met at Falcon Lumber, where they worked together. At that time, one of Frank's employers argued that Frank's last name, Ekstein, sounded too Jewish and asked him to change it to the more Anglo-sounding Richards. Frank absolutely refused to comply and later left the company to work at Weston Road Lumber. Frank eventually took over Weston Road Lumber, which remains a family business today.

Henry Seldon played a central role in Frank's life and was very supportive of our relationship. As a young man, Henry kept busy dating several girls. One of the girls was my friend Helen. Unfortunately, her mother spoiled the relationship by interfering too much. Eventually Henry met Mary, a Holocaust survivor who had experienced the war in Hungary with her mother and brother. Henry and Mary got married six months before Frank and I did. Henry died a few years ago, and Mary and I remain friends.

During the summer of 1952, Frank went with Henry to visit Henry's parents in Cornwall, Ontario. While he was away, I went out to dinner with my aunt, uncle and Tamara, and on the way home we were in a car accident: we were hit so hard that our car spun around. There were no seat belts in cars at that time, and I fell out of the back door, hit my head on a curb and ended up in the hospital with a concussion and forty-two stitches in my head. When I came to, the doctors informed me that I had been unconscious for two days. The crown of my head had been shaved around the stiches, and it took a long time for my hair to grow out. In the meantime, I wore a cap to hide the bald spot. The surgeon charged 150 dollars, a small fortune in those days. After Frank and I were married, we paid this off at the rate of ten dollars a month.

By this time, my aunt and uncle had bought a house at 132 Pendrith Street, just north of Bloor Street and west of Christie Street. We all lived on the main floor: my aunt and uncle slept in the dining room, and Tamara, who now went by Terry, and I slept on a pull-out bed in the living room. The three upstairs rooms were rented out to board-ers. When one of the renters moved out, I asked if I could have the room for the fifteen dollars a week that I was giving my aunt for room and board. I was nearly eighteen and needed a little space of my own. My aunt agreed, and I had a room of my own for the first time since I was a little girl. I was so neat that every time Terry came upstairs to rifle through my drawers, I knew she had been there. "How do you know?" she asked, and I responded that it was obvious she had touched everything; nothing was the way I kept it. I didn't like her touching my things, and I found her annoying, like I imagine most little sisters must be.

Most of the time, my uncle Jack was this quiet, meek man who agreed to everything Auntie Sally said. She ran the house. Uncle didn't talk — he blew up, and when he exploded, all of us felt it. In these fits of anger, he hit Terry, but never me. Once, when we were living on Queen Street, he chased me outside of the house, and I threatened to call the police if he touched me. Experiencing the con-centration camps and the death camps and losing his first wife had crushed Uncle Jack's spirit and left him traumatized. When, in later years, my children asked him about the number tattooed on his arm, he answered that it was his phone number. He was broken, a shell of a man. In Toronto, Auntie Sally was the strong one. She was gracious, a social woman who had many greenie friends and cooked her famous pierogi for anyone who dropped by.

Auntie was the centre of the home, but she and Uncle Jack were both damaged, and it was not a happy marriage. Of all the people they could have met, they found each other. Terry and I suffered greatly, and I stayed away from home as much as possible. I had this idealized vision of my father and thought that if he had survived the Holocaust, he would have known how to raise me properly, with the right balance of discipline and love. Uncle Jack did not know how to achieve that balance with Terry, and their relationship was very strained. I could not understand this at the time, but I realize now that since she was separated from him at such a young age, there was no opportunity for them to have bonded.

One day my aunt met her old friend Herta Getzler on the streets of Toronto. They had both been at Oskar Schindler's factory during the war and in fact had shared a bunk. Herta was living in North Bay and suggested that Uncle Jack might be able to get a job there. He was still finding it difficult to hold down a job, and his income, which was always a big stressor, was only getting worse. So, Auntie, Uncle and Terry moved to North Bay, Ontario. I refused to go. I was an eighteen-year-old working woman with a close group of friends and a boyfriend. After much arguing, it was decided that I would stay in the house. Terry was six years younger than me and had no choice but to go. It was the worst possible decision for the three of them.

Living alone in North Bay with her parents, Terry began to appreciate having a sister, and she started to miss me. Life in North Bay was not only difficult for Terry but for Aunt Sally as well. Toronto had treated Aunt Sally decently, despite the difficulties of her marriage. She had many friends and her work at the Spadina shop, was physically healthy and had a full life. But in North Bay, everything went downhill. Her survivor community all but disappeared; there were only two other Polish Jewish families — Herta Getzler's and the Metzs — with young children. They all led busy lives and had no time for my aunt. The community of native-born Canadians wanted nothing to do with the newcomers and completely ignored her. It was at this point that my aunt experienced the first of several nervous breakdowns. She had lost two children, a husband, parents, sisters, nieces and nephews — the pain and suffering finally caught up with her. From this point on, my aunt was regularly sick and underwent many rounds of electroshock therapy.

And then, while Sala, Jack and Terry were living in North Bay, the secret of Terry's parentage came unravelled. The story goes that my aunt let the truth slip to a neighbour, who passed along the information to her own child. This child, in turn, told Terry. While she always knew that we were not biological sisters, she had no idea that Aunt Sala was not her biological mother. When Terry heard this, she fled to the train station with every intention of travelling to see me in Toronto, but the police caught up with her first and took her home. Tamara was devastated and terribly angry, not only with Jack and Sala, but with me as well. Why did I not tell her, my sister, the truth? How could I keep such an awful secret from her? I told her that I had been threatened into silence and apologized profusely.

With my family gone, every room except mine was rented out to strangers. At one point, two brothers moved in with one of their wives. Every morning when the men left for work, the wife was locked inside their bedroom. At the time, I didn't realize how potentially dangerous it was for me as a young woman alone in this situation. I was young and naive. Since my room had no lock, I used to place a chair under the doorknob to keep the door shut whenever I was in the room. I was very afraid.

I used to tell Frank that I was scared of the tenants and did not like living on my own, but there was no choice. We could not live together as an unmarried couple — my aunt and his parents would have had a fit. This was the 1950s, and my aunt was worried about me. She just wanted me to get married because that's what good Jewish girls did. They married boys with good jobs, made babies and got on with their lives. "What will people say?" my aunt probed whenever Frank came over to watch the television he had bought for my bedroom. She was unhappy about the arrangement, even though our good friends would be there watching television with Frank and me.

The pressure of trying to please our families placed us in an awkward situation, and let me tell you, it was no fun. At one point a mutual acquaintance of my aunt's phoned Frank's parents to inquire about their son's intentions concerning me. My future in-laws were very upset, as was Frank. I was terribly embarrassed. To make my aunt happy, Frank borrowed money from Henry and bought me an engagement ring. The proposal wasn't a big production, and he didn't get down on one knee. Frank and I drove to North Bay to surprise my aunt with the ring. While we planned to marry as soon as possible, the timing wasn't right. Frank and I hoped be more financially established before revealing our engagement to his parents, and I wore the ring on a chain inside my shirt so no one would see it — not the usual way to get engaged.

Frank's parents eventually accepted that we were serious about each other and offered to help him buy me a ring. What were we to do? I returned the ring to Frank. One Friday night in mid-1954, Frank's parents invited me for dinner, and Frank presented me with my ring. I had to pretend to be surprised! It was the greatest performance of my life. When Frank escorted me home, I cried and cried, it was all so terrible. Something that should have been so happy was marred by a lie. But I loved Frank and was excited for the life we would build together.

~

I never forgot the Matusiewiczes and corresponded with them regularly from the time I moved to Toronto. When Lusia got engaged to an older man that her family approved of, I mailed her a gown for the wedding. Though Auntie did not forbid me from speaking to them, I know she hoped I had forgotten about my rescuers — and their religion. Naturally I informed Josef and Lusia of my upcoming marriage to Frank. Josef sent me a special gift from Kluczbork in celebration of my nuptials: the falsified birth certificate that had enabled my survival some years before. The certificate was accompanied by a letter dated May 2, 1955:

*Dear Haneczka,*

*Your letters make us happy. It seems that your heart has not changed toward us.*

*We are very happy that when there is an important event in your life, you let us know. It shows that between us is a bond, more than that of family — when family could not help you in those tragic days when you were faced with death, God sent you a family who saved you. How difficult this was only God knows, but this passed, and you together with us are alive and are not in the same grave. We are very moved by the news of your marriage.*

*When we speak about you, we remember a little girl, like a bird, who flew to us, finding safety under our roof from those who wanted to take [her] life. She stayed a while, rested a little, and again flew into the world, far over seas and mountains to find a new life, to find a friend and husband to go through life with.*

*We wish you on your new path of life health and happiness and blessings from God in every step and luck in everything.*

*Dear Haneczka, we too are sending you a wedding present. Take good care of it...like a talisman [and] souvenir for the future. It is only a small paper card, but how important it was for you. If not for it, there would not be Haneczka today and family and everyone else would have forgotten about her.*

*Today, I am sure you will understand how important this birth cer-tificate was for you in those times. Everything was done the Christian way, not for payment. God helped us in this work. I am sure you can remember when they [the police] came for you. It's as if God put an invisible cover on you, and I was able to take you to Liczkowce because of that piece of paper.*

*With this birth certificate you were legally registered as a cousin of the priest, and you lived legally until you left. It is easy to write this, but living through those times cost us our health. I have problems with my nerves and my liver. When we sometimes think about your survival, we think your parents must have had great help from God and must have prayed for your life.*

*To end, we are sending you the birth certificate and sending you and wishing the young couple once again good luck in your new life journey.*

*J. Matusiewicz with the entire family*

Josef's poetic, sincere words touched my heart. This brave soul risked his life twice to rescue me from imminent danger. I knew he was proud of me and loved me as though I were his real niece. It pleased me tremendously to receive his blessing as I embarked on this new journey with Frank.

# The Challenges and Joys of Motherhood

Wedding planning was no simple task for two immigrant kids. We had no money and did not expect Frank's parents or Auntie Sally to pay for our wedding. Frank and I made all the arrangements ourselves since his mother did not offer to help and my aunt was unwell. So we began to plan, selecting a date in June 1955 and booking the hall at the Borochov Centre on Lippincott Street. My aunt had other plans: she wanted us to have a big wedding and pay for it from the money we might get as gifts. Frank and I were not prepared to go out on a limb and count on funds we did not yet have. After much arguing and aggravation, Frank and I won. I had invitations printed and sent out. A friend went with me to buy a wedding dress — not a gown, just a white lace dress. I also bought a dress for Terry, who was my maid of honour. Little Cheryl Zeiler was my flower girl, and Frank's brother, Paul, was his best man. Jean Zeiler offered their home for last-minute preparations. Ruzia, my aunt and uncle's tenant, had her husband photograph the event. Thanks to him we have a beautiful wedding album. Before leaving for the ceremony, Frank covered me with a veil borrowed from his cousin Midge.

Frank and I were married on June 5, 1955, by Rabbi Slonim. The wedding cost us five hundred dollars, a considerable sum at the time. The ceremony was planned for 3:00 p.m. on a Sunday afternoon so that we didn't have to provide a dinner. Instead, we had a lovely sweet table. In the wedding pictures, you can see guests around that table

— they were like locusts, gobbling up the food! In his excitement, my father-in-law had gone up and down College Street and invited the cleaner, the shoe maker, the barber — everyone he saw! There were so many people I didn't know at my wedding. My family came in from New York: Sylvia and Ted, Pearl and Saul, Renee and Phil, Aunt Esther, Uncle Eli and Aunt Dorothy. Michael stayed at home.

It was the happiest day of my life but also bittersweet. As I waited to walk down the aisle, I cried. I cried because I was an orphan, and Aunt Sally, the closest I had to a mother, had just come out of the hospital after some electroshock treatments and looked terrible. She looked like she was going to a funeral and said she would not give me away because "she had no *mazel*" and was unwell. And so, as we were lined up and waiting, I cried, wishing that my parents could be there. My mother-in-law whispered to me, "Why are you crying? You got what you wanted." I was under so much pressure to please everyone that I became paralyzed. Sensing my nerves and having overheard the comment of my mother-in-law, Anna (or Oma, as I later called her), Sheila, a friend from high school who was acting as my bridal consultant, pushed me forward and ordered, "Just go!" I asked my cousins Sylvia and Ted to walk me down the aisle since Aunt Sally refused. Leo Spellman, a Polish survivor and cousin of the famous pianist Władysław Szpilman (the protagonist in the film *The Pianist*) played the accordion, and our cousins held up the chuppah. It was a beautiful party, but it was over before we knew it. My mother-in-law proceeded to invite her family over for dinner. My relatives were explicitly excluded from the invitation. Aunt Sally, Uncle Jack and Terry got in their car and returned to North Bay. The rest of my family headed home to New York State. Unfortunately, my family and Frank's never grew close.

Frank and I left on our honeymoon straight after the wedding in his brother Paul's car. Before we could take off, we were greeted with an unwanted surprise: the car was decorated with chalk and shaving cream, streamers and the words "Just Married." It was a disaster! I was so embarrassed by the spectacle of it all. I was a private person and felt uncomfortable with the whole world knowing our business. But instead of wiping off the mess, we grinned and bore it, stopping to clean the car in Oshawa. Only then could I relax and start enjoying our trip. Frank and I spent two weeks sightseeing in New York, Lake Placid and Washington, D.C. It was a beautiful honeymoon but hot! Naturally, there was no air conditioning, but all we cared about was being together.

Shortly before our marriage Frank and I purchased a small bungalow at 211 Haddington Avenue. The down payment was six thousand dollars: Frank had saved three thousand, and his father lent us the balance. We repaid the loan within two years. The house was such a mess! The kids who had lived there had punched holes in the bathroom wall over the bathtub. Frank and I spent every weekend for two months before the wedding painting inside and outside and scrubbing all the floors and windows. A funny story about the kitchen: When Frank and I first viewed the property, the floor looked black. Not the nicest, but fine for us. Frank and Paul took it upon themselves to scrub the kitchen floor with brushes, and lo and behold, the floor was actually green! The dirt left by the former occupants was worse than we thought. From here, we began our life as newlyweds.

After two weeks on our east coast honeymoon, Frank and I slept in our marital home for the first time. I felt so lucky to have a husband who loved me and whom I loved with all my heart. It was a wonderful year. Over time we made the house a home. Frank's parents bought us a bedroom set, and we bought a refrigerator, stove and a couch. Our friends gave us a kitchen table and chairs. Frank made a bookcase, and we hired someone to carpet the living room floor. I fulfilled my old promise to have many shoes, and Frank built me a large cupboard with wide shelves to store my growing shoe collection. Every time I looked at it, I told him, "That's my security blanket." Other women collected jewellery, but all I wanted was shoes. When you don't have something for such a long time and you get it, you cling to it.

Our home was small and cozy. In our first year of marriage Frank taught me to drive. I was a difficult student. One time, I took the ramp onto the highway and refused to continue driving. I was scared and he was frustrated. It did not go well. But when I took my driving exam, I managed to pass, and I was able to come home and show Frank my new licence. Like I had done many times before, I had overcome my fears. That same year, I turned twenty-one and could apply for Canadian citizenship. I don't remember being especially excited by the prospect; after all, I had already been living in Canada for seven years and considered myself Canadian. I was mostly just happy to no longer be stateless.

~

Since his return from Siberia, I had been pressing Josef for details about my father's death to no avail. I suppose he was trying to protect me, his little niece, from the grim details of what was certainly a terrible event. In a letter dated April 6, 1956, Josef reflected on our escape from Synowódzko Wyżne and shared updates on the family:

*Kochana Haneczka,*

*I did not write to you because it is difficult for me to write. But today I made myself write because today is [more than] ten years since I ran with you in the night from Synowódzko, very afraid that we would be caught by our enemies.*

*And afterwards, at the train station in Mikołów, you had to pretend that you were ill, because a Ukrainian policeman whom I knew was also there. Today we can laugh about this, isn't that true? But it was not funny then, when life was at stake. Then, [we escaped] thanks to a good train conductor who allowed us to go with him (not a passenger train) — and everywhere our enemies, Germans and Ukrainians, who could have stopped us. And what would have happened if they stopped us? Today we need not think about this. God helped us avoid all the problems, and we arrived safely to Liczkowce to Father Michal. And then things were quieter, yes, Haneczka, ten years[3] is not such a long time, but a lot has changed since then. I remember you as a little girl, and today you are married and soon will be a mother, happy with life. You have a good husband, and you work together so that your life should be happy and lucky. What was ten years? We should pretend that it was a very bad dream that will never return.*

*With us, Lusia already has two children who do with their grandfather [Josef] whatever they want because Grandfather loves them and tells them stories. Basia, with whom you played, is now a young lady, finishing high school and going on to university to become an engineer. If you were here you would have finished university by now because it is free and paid for by the country, so anyone can attend. But for you it is better where you are because you have family, and here you would be lonely. Ala, Basia's younger sister, is in Grade 9 and is taller than Basia. I have also changed. Soon I will be seventy years old, and after what I lived through in the camps, I need to have a serious operation soon. I love and enjoy the children, and the fact that I did something good in my life by saving the life of a little orphan. Maybe there on the other side it will be counted. We have to thank God because without his help we could not have done it.*

*Father Michal is close to us and sometimes he writes. As always he is at a church. Karola is not with him because she was a terrible woman. She caused a lot of trouble for us. She was convicted and spent one and a half years in jail.[4] I don't know where she is now, and I don't think about that witch.*

*I will finish now and send you and your husband, Aunt Sally and all of your relatives best regards. God should bless you and help you in every step of your life. This is the wish of your old uncle.*

*Josef Matusiewicz*

---

3  Josef brought Anita to the parish in May 1943, so this letter would have been written closer to thirteen years after that event.

4  It is unclear what Karola was convicted of.

But there was still no word about my father's death. Finally, more than a year after my wedding, I learned the truth. In a letter dated October 20, 1956, and addressed to Frank, Josef began with a warning: Do not allow Anita to read the letter by herself. So, with a heavy heart, Frank and I read the letter together.

*Kochana Haneczka,*

*I received the slippers, they are very good, and I thank you very much for them. The medicine is good during the attacks and helps with the pain. The nebulizer [puffer] broke, but I hope it can be fixed.*

*Nothing new with us — we are working around the house so we can live. We live at number 18, not 16 where you lived with us, and even from here they want to evict us because the German owner came back. Where we will go, we do not know. We are like nomads, always moving. But that is how it is. Somehow God will help. We had worse times, isn't that true? And we are still living. Of course, this too shall pass.*

*Haneczka, you write that you want to know about your father. What should I write you? Should I write about the terrible event that befell innocent people? It is terrible to return to those times, especially when it is about your parents. But since you want to know, I will tell you about your father and his end.*

*You probably remember that your father was an accountant in a mill in Synowódzko Wyżne, near Skole. You lived within your means but very nicely. All your belongings were left with your landlords, but the Ukrainians would not give him even your clothes — but that is not important.*

*Your father spoke English, German, Hebrew, Polish and Russian. He wore very strong eyeglasses. He was a good man — quiet, honest, trustworthy, he did not know of falsehoods. A person like that is difficult to find today. We talked to each other a lot. During our conversations, he was very interested in Catholicism and said that after the war he would be inclined to change his religion. And he said that we should raise you as a Catholic.*

*In 1942, they took your mother together with thousands of others.*

[Then you were in] *a house in Hochtief — I am sure that you remember that dirty, dark room. I tried to get food for you when I could. Seeing your father's desperation, I ran away with you in the night to my family, and when it got to be very bad, I ran away with you to Liczkowce to Father Michal. These were very bad times for you and for us. But, thank God, this too passed and we managed to save you. You probably remember most of this.*

*And now, dear Haneczka, I have to write about the last act of the terrible tragedy of your father — even though your father was a little responsible for what took place. I was constantly telling him to run away. He could have done it because he could get money, and it was easy to get bread. Unfortunately, he believed that the German Heutuschke* [the commandant] *Bauleiter* [site manager] *of Hochtief would protect him. He also did not want to leave* [his friend] *Artek Horowitz, and he could not run away with him.*

*This lasted until July, and your father kept putting off running away. On the critical day, when I came to the warehouse as usual, I found out that in Skole, all those Jews who were still alive were killed. Only three were left in Synowódzko: your father, Artek and Schreiben, I think that was his name. Artek was already locked up, Schreiben was still free. I could not phone your father because many Germans were there. I could not phone from the post office because I was afraid of the postmaster. I told Schreiben the whole story and asked him to immediately tell your father. Unfortunately, he did not do this. He kept walking around until he was also locked up. In the meantime, I heard the order to shoot the three people. Your father heard the word "schiessen"* [shoot] *spoken by the German* [named] *Meyer, and he still could have run. But he did not do that; only when they came to lock him up did he try to run into the Stryj River. Unfortunately, Ukrainian workers went after him to catch him. Your father walked and swam in the river for three hours, but they would not let him get close to the woods. Eventually, your father got tired, and then they caught him, and at around 5:00 p.m. they shot all three. They buried them on land near the train tracks, nine metres from semaphore* [railway signalling post] *toward the tunnel and nine metres toward the town.*

*I came from my job in the warehouse and went straight to your father, thinking there was still some time to save him, but unfortunately, I saw him only from far away standing in the water. Only night could save him, but it was still far away.*

*I am sorry, Haneczka, that you forced me to write this letter. Maybe now that you know the truth you will not think so much about it, and maybe forget it.*

*Best regards to both of you,*

*Josef Matusiewicz*

It was painful to read these words. I was grateful to finally know what had happened to my father and that his death was no longer shrouded in mystery and what-ifs. But I had an extremely difficult time understanding his response to the increasingly precarious situation at Hochtief camp. Why didn't he try to escape when he had the chance? He knew the nearby forest so well. According to Josef, it seemed that my father believed that he was invaluable to the site and that the German commandant would protect him. Indeed, my father was an asset to the Germans, which likely explains how he survived that long and why our family had been spared deportation two years earlier.

I wondered whether my father felt an allegiance to his fellow Jewish prisoners, Artek and Schreiben. Did they make a pact to stick together? Did one of them prevent the others from fleeing? What was he going to do alone in the woods? The idea of running into the unknown must have been terrifying. It would have been nearly impossible to survive without help. In those parts, some Jewish escapees joined up with partisans, but many others were killed right away by Ukrainians. Did my dear father know his death was imminent?

I will never know what was going through his mind as he ran, or what he experienced when the Ukrainian workers shot him. I pray he didn't suffer too much. Maybe knowing that I was safe with Josef brought my father some solace. I certainly hope so.

Josef passed away a short time after sending the letter. Did he sense he was approaching the end of his life? Perhaps this is why he decided to finally disclose the painful scene he witnessed those years before. Thank goodness he did. As painful as it was to learn about my father's final moments, I am eternally grateful that they did not die with Josef, his dear friend and my personal saviour.

While I was devastated by the news of Josef's death, I did not allow it to paralyze me. On June 8, 1957, Frank and I welcomed our first child, a son named Richard Fred, or Ricky, as we called him. We gave him the Hebrew name Fischel, after my late father, and the name Fred, after Frank's uncle who had recently died. Frank and I were delighted, and I was finally able to have the family that I craved. Everyone doted on Ricky. By this time my in-laws lived around the corner from us. Every night when I was trying to put Ricky to bed, they would visit and get him all riled up. Sometimes they would watch me give him a bath, but mostly they just made him crazy and then went home, and I was always left to calm him down and get him to bed. For three years Ricky was an only child, spoiled by everyone. He was very smart, learned quickly and was a busy little boy. Our daughter, Ruthie, joined us three years later on June 1, 1960. We named her Ruth Elaine in memory of my mother, Edzia, or Ettel Rivka.

Frank and I thought that our family was complete. By this time Frank was already working for Weston Road Lumber, a Jewish-owned lumber company located on railroad property at Weston Road near St. Clair Avenue. When the company was given notice to move, Frank was charged with finding a new location. He looked around and eventually settled on a lot on Torbram Road, in Mississauga. The company commissioned a new building, and Weston Road Lumber moved to its new location in 1970.

It was not easy for Frank. His boss, Mr. Szusz, who was a partner in the business, gave him a very hard time. We did not have much money, but we managed to get by and even save a little. Little by little, Frank purchased shares from the business partners. After proving himself to be a valuable employee, Mr. Szusz gave Frank an old company car. This dramatically shortened his commute, which allowed him to spend more time at home. This was especially fortunate because sixteen months after Ruth came into this world, our third child was born, sooner than we had planned. Peter arrived on September 29, 1961. Frank and I called him our sunshine child because he was such a happy and good little boy. We were thrilled to have him. I had always wanted to have four children, but after three C-sections my doctor said "enough."

The first year of Peter's life was difficult. We had two babies in diapers. There were no disposable diapers then, and there was such a thing as diaper service, but we couldn't afford it. I owned a wringer washer that my aunt and uncle had bought for us, but no dryer. In the summer, I hung everything on a line outside, but in the winter I used clotheslines that were strung up in the basement. Frank and I spent evenings folding diapers. While the kids slept, I did bookkeeping for my brother-in-law Paul's company. One day Paul took pity on me and bought me the greatest gift I've ever received: a dryer. That dryer saved my life, and my arms from all that hanging!

Before Peter was born, my aunt, uncle and Terry returned to Toronto from North Bay. Terry had had an awful time up north; she was isolated and lonely, and Frank and I had even talked about having her live with us. She was still very angry about having been lied to about her true parentage for all those years. She felt that I had betrayed her trust by withholding such critical information and felt hurt that I, her sister, had caused her such pain. It took a long time for her to forgive me, and for us to repair our relationship. Today we are very close, and my children call her Auntie Terry. We speak all the time and try to visit regularly. Our relationship is the best thing to come out of Sala and Jack's marriage.

When they came back to Toronto, my aunt and uncle bought a variety store in Mimico, Etobicoke, right near the lake. My aunt continued to suffer from nervous breakdowns and had several sessions of shock therapy treatments. She asked me to be in the hospital room with her while she had a treatment. It was an awful sight. I didn't know it at the time, but I was pregnant with Peter, and I passed out during the session. Her psychiatrist was in the room and told me to see a doctor. The experience was devastating, and I refused to accompany her to future treatments. During this difficult time, Frank was so wonderful to us all, and he assumed responsibility for taking my aunt to her shock treatments nearly every month. He would then bring my startled and confused aunt back to our home to sleep and recover. It was like having a fourth kid to look after.

Those early years were very difficult for my entire family. When I think of that time now, I don't know how I managed not to have a nervous breakdown of my own. Aunt Sally was so sick and depressed, going in and out of the hospital. This remained the unfortunate pattern until Uncle Jack passed away in 1980. Then, miraculously, she was healthy again. They were just so harmful to each other.

I had always craved a family of my own and could not wait to be a mother, but boy, it was not easy! With the exception of Frank's support after his own long days at work, I had no help whatsoever. I could not afford a cleaning lady, and with three little kids, there was always a mess of toys all over the living room. I worked very hard to keep it clean and orderly. My mother-in-law was not helpful and quite cold toward me. She never treated me like a daughter, a role I would have been happy to assume. I was usually exhausted and never got enough sleep. Peter slept in a crib in our bedroom, and when he woke at night, I would take him to the living room to feed him so that the other children and Frank could sleep. Then I would rock the carriage until he fell asleep again.

Despite my aunt's busy schedule at the variety store and her constant illnesses, she helped out whenever she was able. When I was in the hospital with Peter after my Caesarean, Frank wanted to surprise me and had the bathroom professionally updated. The workers left the bathroom a mess. Guess who came to clean things up? Auntie Sally. She left her responsibilities at the store and took care of everything. She knew I would have a fit if I came home from the hospital and saw the mess in the bathroom, never mind the fact that I had a Caesarean and could not get on my hands and knees to wash the floor. I was forever grateful for Auntie's help and thoughtfulness.

When the weather cooperated, I took the children on a daily walk: Peter in the carriage, Ruthie sitting on a seat across the bottom of the carriage, and Ricky walking alongside holding on to the carriage or me. Some days we walked all the way to Lawrence Avenue and window-shopped. Thankfully the children slept a couple of hours every afternoon so I could get things done around the house. I served a homemade dinner every night, learning to make Czech dishes from my mother-in-law. Grocery shopping took place in the evenings when I could use the car. We had no money for luxuries like restaurant dining.

By this time, my Central Commerce girlfriends were all married with babies of their own. It was difficult to get together: I didn't have a car of my own or anyone to watch the kids. Yet our friendships continue to this day. Some of our kids also became friendly, though for the most part Rick, Ruth and Peter mainly played outside with the neighbourhood kids. Ruthie was so competitive, she used to run like the wind and play sports with the boys. Once she started running and performing better than them, they kicked her out. They didn't want to play with a girl anymore. It was crazy how my sons tormented her, but my daughter is a strong one and put them in their place. Nobody ever bossed her around.

Shortly after we moved to Haddington Avenue, I met Ethel Landis. She lived on the same street as me and became my closest friend. Ethel, like my other friends, felt that I completely fit into the crowd, that there was nothing different about me, nothing depressing; I was upbeat and fun. Although she knew I was a Holocaust survivor, we simply did not speak about my Holocaust experiences. Ethel became more sensitive to what I had gone through when she saw Aunt Sally's often difficult behaviour toward me. But it was over two decades before she heard about my hiding in the wardrobe at Hochtief and about my other experiences. I opened up about my family, the Matusiewiczes and my years as a hidden child only in the 1980s and 1990s, following the rise of public consciousness about the Holocaust and in my new role as an educator. Ethel remains my closest friend to this day.

Inside our home, Jewish traditions and Zionistic values were alive and well. In many ways, I made Frank Jewish since he was raised with nearly no religion at all. My secular father-in-law was one of the original founding members of Congregation Habonim, a liberal synagogue for mostly Central European refugees and survivors, so naturally Frank and I joined upon our marriage. During the first two years of our marriage, holiday celebrations were really hectic. At Passover, for example, we first had to go to my in-laws for dinner, as they did not make a seder. The same evening, we had to schlep to Mimico for a seder with my aunt and uncle. This went on until Rick was born. I finally became fed up and announced that I was not going to do it anymore. I began making the seder and inviting both of our families. I continued hosting seders for my children and grandchildren until a few years ago, when my daughter took over hosting duties.

We belonged to Congregation Habonim until Rick was old enough to attend Hebrew school. We wanted our children to have a Jewish education but could not afford the tuition at Associated Hebrew School. Since Habonim did not offer Hebrew school classes, we joined Beth David and drove Rick to class three times a week. Ruth and Peter also attended classes there. I remain an active member of the congregation today.

By this time, I had shed all connections to Catholicism save my regular communication with the Matusiewiczes. As soon as Frank and I were married and had a little bit of money, we began sending packages to Poland. We sent jeans, medication, coffee, cocoa — there was a terrible shortage of basic supplies under Communism, and everything helped. I was so embarrassed by my Polish and sure that I was making terrible mistakes in my letters, even though Josef and Lusia claimed they understood my notes. It was Lusia who wrote to inform me when her aunt and uncle passed away in 1947 and 1957, respectively. My dear rescuer had one simple request: to hold a Mass in their memory. I had been too young to organize anything, let alone a church service, when Paulina died. But Josef's death affected me differently. I went to a Catholic church near Wilson Avenue and Avenue Road and asked the priest to say Mass for Paulina and Josef. I owed my protectors, my angels, this much. Nobody asked questions, and I probably would not have told the priest anyhow. Even though I had been baptized and was eligible to attend Mass, I left before the service. I did all that I could do. I was now Jewish through and through.

When Rick started school, I got involved by writing the school bulletin. I did this for several years. And I was still doing bookkeeping for Frank's brother, Paul. Frank and his brother were very close and saw each other often. In later years, Frank would stop at Paul's farm practically every day on his way to work. We were close to Paul, his wife, Nili, and their sons, Steve and Ari, who were quite a bit younger than our kids. Our families lived on the same street for several years, and Frank and the kids walked over there quite often. Today, the cousins all maintain close relationships.

These years were ones of adjustment for Terry. She visited our home frequently, and it became a refuge for her. Her parents were both unwell and had a hard time coping with a teenager. They were also working incredibly hard at their convenience store fifteen hours a day. Terry was the only Jewish student in a very Christian neighbourhood, and our support gave her a sense of security, which she is still grateful for to this day.

Terry finished high school and enrolled at the University of Toronto. Unfortunately, we could not help her financially, but Frank and I were her biggest supporters. She would spend time in our home when she needed a moment of peace. Needless to say, my aunt and uncle were not pleased. They wanted Terry to work in the store after school and on weekends. It was a moving moment for us when Terry went off to graduate school at the University of Illinois at Urbana-Champaign. I took her to the train station, and as we waited for her train, I told her that I was afraid she might leave forever. But Terry assured me that we would remain close. I phoned Terry every Sunday while she was in graduate school, even though long-distance calls were expensive.

Terry earned her master's degree and then pursued a PhD in sixteenth-century French literature. She met her husband, Michael Root, during their master's studies. Upon finishing their doctorates, both secured teaching positions in Minnesota: Michael at University of Minnesota and Terry at Hamline University in Saint Paul. They both taught for thirty years and are now retired. I am very proud of Terry. We have a warm and loving relationship and see each other as much as possible.

∼

I adored being a mother and was always actively involved in my children's lives. However, as much as I loved them, I desperately needed some adult conversation; until Frank came home after work, I spoke only with the kids. So, once Peter started kindergarten, I became involved with an organization called Senior Care, delivering Kosher Meals on Wheels to house-bound Jewish seniors. The flexible morning schedule one day a week allowed me to be back in time to serve the kids lunch at home. This was the start to a lifetime of volunteering.

I delivered Meals on Wheels once or twice a week for several years. In 1980, I was elected to sit on the Senior Care Executive Committee as vice president of volunteers and was appointed to chair the

Volunteer Advisory Committee for the next four years. I remained a board member of Senior Care for ten years. Today, I am still active with Senior Care, which is now called Circle of Care. I sit on their committee that works with the Claims Conference (The Conference on Jewish Material Claims Against Germany), which distributes reparation money to Holocaust survivors. I became involved because the committee needed survivors on it. We meet about once a month and discuss cases of survivors in the community who require dental care, sleeping devices, and nursing and health support services. There was once even a request for a tombstone. That one nearly killed me. It was devastating to know that my peers, other survivors, could not afford to put up a tombstone. This is very important work, and I cannot say no to somebody who genuinely needs help.

Once all the kids were attending school full time, I became involved with the Home and School Association and joined the National Council of Jewish Women's Downsview study group. Frank stayed home with the kids at night so that I could get out of the house and make new friends. I loved the programming that the study group organized on art, literature and current events. It was interesting and stimulating, and I learned a great deal. I was a member of the study group for many years and took on different positions. Elaine Newton, a professor at York University, was our group advisor, and she and I became close friends. Many years after we met, she was instrumental in my admission to York University as a mature student on the strength of my two years of high school plus my community service. I was very surprised and excited to be accepted.

I had always wanted to pursue higher education but had left high school early to help support my family. I enrolled at York University as a mature student while Ricky was completing his first degree. I think he was embarrassed to have his mother there; every time he saw me coming, he hid behind a newspaper. It took me a long time to finish because I still had children to raise and a home to run. While I was studying, Peter also started at York. Unlike his brother, Peter would see me from a distance and call out, "Hi, Mom!" and come over to talk to me. The young students in my classes used to ask me, "What are you doing here? What do you want to do this for?" I responded that I had missed out on the opportunity to get a higher education when I was younger. Frank never made it to university because he needed to work, but he had at least completed high school. Frank was a voracious reader all his life and a very intelligent man and was very up to date on various subjects. He was very proud and supportive of my studies and joked that he put four kids through university!

Going to university surrounded by younger students did not bother me. I took my classes seriously and went straight home after school to write. Since my kids and I were getting degrees at the same time, not only did I have to write and type my own essays, I also had to type theirs! I always used to ask them why they waited until the last minute to get things done. All of this studying and writing took place in the evenings, so poor Frank was left to his own devices. My busy schedule meant that we could only take vacations during Christmas or reading week, but we preferred to spend time with the kids. It was a pretty difficult time but very rewarding. Despite the challenges, when I think back on those years, I remember them as being the happiest. Frank was a wonderful husband and father and helped a lot in the evenings and on the weekends. Frank always loved horses and sought out opportunities to ride. He had Ricky on a horse before he could even walk. In his later years, Frank owned four horses and continued to ride whenever he could. It was a beautiful, blessed life. Frank and I successfully built the family I never had, and I cherished every minute.

In June 1985, Peter and I graduated from York University on the same day: Peter with a master of business administration, and me with a bachelor of arts in psychology. Somebody — probably Frank —·phoned the *Toronto Star*, and a reporter published an article about the two of us graduating together.

Frank and I tried to give our children rich and meaningful life experiences, which perhaps explains why I rarely spoke with them about my own childhood. The kids knew that I had been in a war and did not have any parents. I do not recall sharing many more details than this. However, Ruthie once found me on the floor in the cupboard, reading my father's letter, crying. My sweet five-year-old daughter asked, "Where are your mommy and daddy?" Frank had parents, after all, so she assumed I did as well. I had to explain to her that they were dead. "Where did they die?" she wondered. I replied simply, "In the war." What else could I say? That was enough. She did not ask more about my parents; she left it alone. When the children asked questions, I answered, but they did not hear the entire story until they were quite a bit older. All I wanted was to shield my children from pain and suffering.

# Returning to My Roots

Frank and I travelled to Poland together for the first time in 1975. We needed visas to enter the country. Unfortunately, Josef and Paulina had died years earlier, but I desperately wanted to see Lusia. She and her family welcomed us into their Kluczbork home with open arms. It was an emotional reunion. We talked and we talked and we talked day and night about the war years and our lives since. Frank had come to understand Polish because he spoke Czech — the two languages are similar — and from hearing me speak with my aunt and uncle in Polish for twenty years. By that time, I also understood Czech, the language Frank's family spoke. In Kluczbork, Frank spoke to Lusia in Czech, and they understood each other well enough to engage in conversation. Lusia described details of my life in hiding and answered many questions, which I believe gave Frank a better understanding of my survival. It meant so much to me that they could spend time with one another.

Thirty years had passed but little had changed in Kluczbork. Life was very difficult for people under Communist rule. Lusia would leave very early in the morning to stand in line to buy bread. The lines went on forever, but the store shelves were empty. People were rude and unhappy because they suffered so greatly and had no power to change the situation. On our visit, Frank and I spent time with Basia and Ala, the daughters of Father Michal's sister. They were very young when I left Poland. Basia accompanied us to the site of the former concentration camp at Auschwitz. When we arrived, we learned that the buildings were all locked, and we were not able to enter. The only thing that mattered, however, was that I saw my Lusia.

On this trip we also went to Aunt Sala's old apartment in Krakow. I recognized it immediately. I knocked on the door, and the elderly woman who opened it claimed to remember me and my mother. Everything inside the apartment was exactly the way I remembered it. All I could think was, "These were my aunt's things." When I returned to Canada, my aunt confirmed my suspicions: the furniture and books had indeed belonged to her. She never wished to return to Poland.

After Poland, we continued to follow my post-war journey and visited Paris. I wanted Frank to see the place where I regained my faith in humanity, reconnected with Judaism and truly began to receive an education. One day I took him to the decrepit building on 26 Avenue d'Italie where Aunt Sally, Uncle Jack and Tamara and I lived. The building had been torn down and replaced with a parking lot. Good riddance — it was awful!

When Ruth and I visited Paris in 1979 to celebrate Ruth's high school graduation, I got in touch with Solange, the kind daughter of the family where I had spent the summer of 1947. After Aunt Sally and I left Europe for Canada, Uncle Jack had arranged for Tamara to live with Solange and her family for several months as well. Tamara had experienced so many changes and adjustments but felt comfortable with Solange. The two communicated regularly for many years. This is how I connected with Solange. Solange joined us in Paris, and we spent a lovely day together. I was pleased to discover that she remained the same caring and special young woman I knew as a child. And excitedly, we communicated in fluent French. I do not know if she is still alive today.

While in Paris, I also took Ruth to the church I used to go to for comfort and we sat there together in silence. Years later, Ruth reflected on that experience: "I imagine I must have felt pretty strange being in a church — the place where my mother ran for comfort — as a Jew. But I know I wasn't uncomfortable. I think I felt grateful that my mother had this beautiful place to run to." Decades later, this feeling remains.

Frank and I spoke often about my desire to go back to see Lwów and my childhood hometown of Synowódzko Wyżne. In 1989, we travelled to Eastern Europe. After the recent fall of Communism, it was finally possible to obtain visas to enter Ukraine. It was a very difficult trip on all accounts. At the time, you could not take a flight directly into Lviv, the current name for Lwów. We booked tickets to Kiev, intending to fly straight from there to Lviv. We spent a couple of days in Kiev, exploring the city. Kiev was depressing. There were many men on the streets asking for money. Frank and I were approached several times, but we were afraid to get involved. I was afraid of Ukrainians in general, remembering how cruel they had been.

We also visited Babi Yar, the site of one of the largest mass murders of Jews at one location during the Holocaust, where over thirty thousand men, women and children were murdered in a ravine northwest of the city in just two days. A monument with a tribute in Hebrew and Ukrainian was erected at the site a few years after our visit. Frank and I said Kaddish, the Jewish prayer for the dead. It was devastating to be in that place. The inhumanity! How could people do this to one another?

Following this visit, we were ready to move on to Lviv. But guess what? There was a strike: no buses, no trains, no planes. What were we going to do? We had travelled such a distance that there was no turning back now. Rather than wait for the strike to end, Frank arranged for a rental car with two Ukrainian drivers. I guess the traumatic experiences of the war were still with me because the entire seven-hour drive I was afraid that the two drivers would take us into the forest and kill us. (I was afraid of Ukrainians because during the war, they had often behaved worse than the Germans, and they were responsible for my father's murder.) The drivers had to take containers of petrol in the car because there was none available for purchase along the highway. I was so relieved when we arrived in Lviv, the city of my birth.

Lviv was a real disaster and just as depressing as Kiev. Although the city had not been destroyed during the war, the once-beautiful buildings were neglected and dirty. The hotel we stayed at was terrible, and it seemed to us that we had the most dark and depressing room in Lviv. I was afraid to go to sleep. The restaurant served food we did not recognize on cracked dishes, and the cups were missing handles. Outside of the hotel things were no better. I couldn't find anything in the city because all the street names had been changed to Ukrainian names. I wanted to find the clinic where I was born, but it was impossible. There were no visible signs of Jewish life, only plaques marking a former Jewish presence, including one at the site of the Janowska concentration camp, where my incredible and intelligent Uncle Chaim (Joachim) Schoenfeld had survived internment.

From there, Frank located another car and driver to take us to Synowódzko Wyżne. It was very tough to go back. No one that I knew remained, and everyone in the town now spoke Ukrainian. Our first stop was the location of my childhood home. I hoped to find our former landlords, Vasil and Paulina Kamionkowie, and retrieve some of our family property that my father had entrusted to them, especially my father's photo albums and stamp collection, but the house had been converted into a post office. Inside, I discovered our tiled stove still standing in the same place, just as I remembered. It was very difficult to return to the home I had shared with my parents and to all the memories we had made there. The tears started to flow.

While wandering along the main street, Frank and I encountered an elderly looking woman who still spoke Polish. We asked her whether she had been there during the first two years of war under the Soviets. She replied that she was not old enough and knew nothing. I suppose the hard living aged people faster. The woman directed us to a Polish-speaking neighbour.

The neighbour invited us into his house. We learned that Vasil and Paulina had both died years earlier; he had no idea what happened to their personal property. Then the man remembered that a Jewish family had once lived in the house. The father was a tall man who wore glasses, and the couple had a little girl. I said, "I am the little girl." The man went on to tell me how the Ukrainian population went on a rampage just before and after the German occupation. But I didn't hear anything he said after he mentioned my family, and I think he was in shock as well. None of it mattered anyways. I couldn't wait to get out of there.

I learned about my maternal grandparents' fates because of a chance meeting in the town of Sambor with an elderly Jewish man who knew my family. He was the only Jew remaining in Sambor; he had no relatives. A lawyer before the war, he survived with the Soviet army, but his family did not survive. He remembered my grandparents and told me how they and other Jews of the town had been murdered: My grandfather was murdered in his bed by a Nazi. After the German occupation in 1941, the new authorities concentrated over six thousand Jews inside the Sambor ghetto. My grandmother was likely among those taken to the Radłowice forest to be shot by the Einsatzgruppen. Out of the eight thousand Jews who lived in Sambor before the war, only about 160 survived.

This man directed us to Radłowice so that we could see the graves. Frank and I took a taxi there but could not find anything. There was an army camp nearby, and when we asked, a young soldier took us to one grave; he did not know of any others. The grave had been dug up by humans or animals. Frank yelled at me, "Don't look!" but it was too late. I had already seen the bones. I was terribly upset, realizing that they could be my relatives' bones. I cried, and Frank and I said Kaddish. On our return to Lviv, we found a synagogue and asked the people there to ensure that the grave be closed up. Frank and I left them some money and told them to let us know when the work was done. We never heard from them. During a March of the Living trip in Krakow years later, we met some people who had just returned from Sambor and Radłowice. They told me that there is now a monument at the Radłowice forest and that the grave is fenced in.

Stryj was also a very difficult place for me to return to. I did not try to find the apartment where my paternal grandparents and my aunt Miriam (Macia) had lived. I knew there was nobody there, as I had been there with Lusia in 1945. Frank and I visited a mass grave outside of Stryj, in a place called Holobutiv. I have no way of knowing if any of my relatives were murdered there. The place that generations of Helfgotts had called home was now bereft of Jews.

Ruthie and I went to Poland in March 1993 with a UJA trip to commemorate the fiftieth anniversary of the Warsaw Ghetto Uprising. We met with Lusia and videotaped her telling her story. She was happy to make the tape, but, fearing repercussions from her antisemitic neighbours, made me promise to not show the recording in Poland during her lifetime. I took Ruthie to Krakow to see the building where Aunt Sally had lived before the war. We did not look inside. I also took her to see and hear the bugler, like my mother had taken me such a long time ago. It was a special moment for the two of us. In 1998, I convinced our March of the Living leader, Barbara Banks, to detour our bus to the church so I could watch the bugler once again. I will never forget that day and the memory of sheer happiness and love.

In the late 1990s, I brought Lusia and her daughter, Marysia, to Toronto for a two-week visit. I was so pleased that Lusia could meet my children and grandchildren and that they could meet her. It was a very special time, filled with laughter and tears. At this meeting, my son Peter pointed toward Lusia and told his eight-year-old daughter, Orli, "See this lady? If it was not for her, neither of us would be here." Orli responded with, "But mommy would be here."

On Sunday morning, I took Lusia and Marysia to Mass at a Polish church on Roncesvalles Avenue. It felt odd being in church with Lusia again, this time as a Jew. Lusia dropped to her knees, looked at me and said, "It is not too late, you can come back." I didn't want to hurt her but politely responded, "No, my parents were Jewish, the family that was left was Jewish, my husband is Jewish. It's what's in my heart." I no longer had to hide my true identity. And yet the church brought back a flood of memories. Lusia went to take Communion, and for a moment I thought, "I was baptized, I could do that." But what for? My belief that the wafer represented the body of Christ had disappeared long ago. I had no need for the little wafer.

Lusia and Marysia spent all their time with us, including Shabbat dinners. I took them to the Holocaust Centre to see an exhibit. But Lusia never gave up hope that I would return to Catholicism. Out of mutual respect, or perhaps awkwardness, Lusia and I never discussed my Catholicism and the beliefs I had clung to during the war. I hope she accepted my decision to be Jewish and was not too disappointed. Since then, Marysia's daughter, Marta, has come to visit Canada, and we consider her part of the family.

In 1998, Frank and I travelled to Poland and Ukraine with our son Rick, Rick's wife, Lillian, and granddaughters Stephanie and Michelle. We wanted them to see where their grandparents and great-grandparents came from. This trip was a little bit easier for me than our first trip. In my mother's birthplace of Sambor, we looked for the synagogue my grandfather had taken me to as a child, but the building had been repurposed as a warehouse. My grandparents' home was also gone and the field across from the property where Roma once kept their caravans now held a school. At the nearby Radłowice forest, we visited the killing site where many of Sambor's Jews were shot and buried in mass graves. Outside of Stryj, we paid our respects in the forest where several family members had been killed. In town, we viewed remnants of the synagogue that was destroyed by the Germans and allowed to rot under Soviet administration. The building had four walls but no roof. What a depressing sight.

The last stop on our tour was Synowódzko Wyżne. Thanks to

identifying features in Josef's letter, we were able to locate the field by the railroad tracks where my father had been killed. As a united family, we walked into the field where my father took his final steps and lit a *yarzheit* (memorial) candle. With heavy hearts we recited Kaddish for my father. It is possible that we were on or near my father's grave. We will never know. On my first trip back, I had been so overcome with emotion that I never thought to ask about the Hochtief camp. This time, I asked some elderly men if they knew where the camp's Jewish forced labourers had lived. We were taken to a large two-storey building, one of only a few in town, now serving as office space. Of course, I had no idea which room my father and I had stayed in; I had never seen the camp in daylight. But now, as I walked down a hallway with my family, Lillian looked through a keyhole and saw a large piece of furniture. There it was! The wardrobe I spent seven weeks hiding inside was still there, although in a state of disrepair. It was a shock to see it again, the place where I had spent seven weeks. The sight of it brought back terrible memories. This is where I said goodbye to my father for the last time. Seeing the room, I became hysterical and could not stop crying. I think I scared everyone, and Frank tried to calm me down. All Rick could ask was, "Mom, how did you ever fit in there?" I replied that I had been eight years old and quite small. Rick wanted to ship the wardrobe to Israel and donate it to Yad Vashem. I absolutely did not want to see it again. This relic was all that remained of the camp.

After our emotionally charged visit to Eastern Europe, we travelled to Prague to show our family the estate where Frank had been born and lived with his parents as a child. The property once boasted a house and barns because my father-in-law was a cattle dealer, but the house was no longer standing, and the barns and property had deteriorated. Where the gardens used to be there were now three new houses. After the war, Frank was told that because his father had not paid taxes since 1939, the house no longer belonged to the family. The prized land was first requisitioned by the Germans and later taken over by the Soviets. Today the land is privately owned.

These trips reminded me of where I came from and how I survived when my parents did not. It was of utmost importance to my family and me to officially recognize the Matusiewicz family's courage and selflessness during the war. Josef, Paulina and Lusia risked their own lives to save me, a little Jewish girl — they deserved to be honoured, even posthumously. I began the process of honouring my rescuers as Righteous Among the Nations through Yad Vashem in the mid-1990s. The first step involved documenting my entire Holocaust narrative and my relationship with my rescuers. It was challenging to corroborate my story — a necessity for the honour to be bestowed — since most of the witnesses to my survival were dead. By this time, Josef, Paulina and Father Michal had already been dead for many years. Father Michal died of a heart attack when he was only in his late forties or fifties. Lusia Młot was the only one in the family still living at that time. Fortunately, my cousin Stefan had met with Josef in Katowice after Aunt Sally found me in Kluczbork, and Stefan provided a letter of attestation, detailing the conditions of my rescue.

The nomination package included the letters from my late father, letters Josef wrote to me, my false birth certificate and photographs from my time at Father Michal's parish. For a long time, Lusia was reluctant to receive the title Righteous Among the Nations. She and I had remained in close contact all those years, and she felt it was unnecessary to receive formal recognition. Under Communism, there was an added fear of repercussions for her family's wartime activities. After the fall of the Iron Curtain, I convinced the very modest Lusia to write to Yad Vashem about her and her aunt and uncle's efforts in saving me. Everyone was thrilled when my nomination was approved.

The Righteous Among the Nations ceremony took place at the Israeli embassy in Warsaw on July 14, 1998. The Israeli emissary in Toronto arranged for the ceremony to coincide with my family's visit to Poland. Lusia, her two daughters and two granddaughters travelled to Warsaw for the ceremony. Her son did not come. Frank, Rick and Lillian, and my granddaughters Stephanie and Michelle accompanied me. Thank God Lusia was still alive to receive the Yad Vashem medal and certificate of recognition from the Israeli ambassador to Poland. I was immensely happy to honour my rescuers in this way. Frank told Lusia the ancient Jewish saying: "When you save one life, you save the world." Lusia was a devout woman, and I think this made her happy. It was a very emotional ceremony, and I was filled with gratitude. Lusia died in 2005 after a long life and passed along her medal to Marysia. Today I have warm relationships with Marysia and Marta Kornacka, who recently completed her medical studies in Poland. I communicate with mother and daughter by email and phone and try to get together with them whenever I travel to Poland. They are very important people in my life and part of the extended Ekstein family.

In 2015, Marta and the granddaughter of another Holocaust survivor's rescuers participated in a special March of the Living ceremony. Marta — who had not attended the ceremony seventeen years earlier — was honoured with flowers and asked to offer a few words about her family, their motivation to save my life and our special relationship. Here is what she said:

*My name is Marta Kornacka, and I am a grandchild of Lusia — Emilia Młot. I was asked a few questions about the family and Lusia's motivation. I was thinking about my great-grandparents and Lusia's motivation in rescuing Anita. From today's perspective it seems to be so natural, the right thing to do. But I think I found the answer. A few months ago, I watched a historically based movie about that part of Poland where they lived before and during World War II. It was a horrifying and brutal documentary, but it showed the truth about that tough and unsafe time, a time when no one knew who was a friend and who was not; who will denounce you first, and which neighbour will come during the night and set fire to your home.*

*I think at that time Josef and Paulina Matusiewicz needed to behave as humans. First, they took care of my Grandma Lusia. Then, when Anita's father asked Josef to take care of Anita, he did not hesitate to act. He also promised to do his best to try to find her relatives scattered around the world after the war. Josef and Paulina knew it would be hard to keep Anita because of her religion, but they did not care about differences. I do believe that this fact was not important for them at all. They made the choice because they believed in the concept that human beings were equal. I also remember Grandma telling me she was teaching Anita the Catholic prayers in Polish so that it would be harder to discover that Anita was Jewish.*

*Nowadays, I know better, and I call them brave people, but I am sure at that time they just had to believe in humanity. They needed to have hope for a better future, and being good made it easier to survive. I never heard my Grandma call herself a hero. Some of us may ask: why did they take the risk to hide Anita? I think there is only one answer: because for them it was the only right option.*

*When my Grandma passed away almost ten years ago, I was sixteen years old. Unfortunately, I did not hear a lot of stories because Poland was not a completely free country from World War II until the 1990s. It is sad, but it was safer for Lusia to keep it as a secret. One of her favourite stories was how she (or Josef) transported Anita [to] hiding... inside an old wooden carriage with hay... Lusia also liked to mention their classes, learning the Polish alphabet, language, songs and prayers. She told me that Anita was really smart and a fast learner. It is very impressive how Anita still knows how to speak Polish very well today.*

*From the memories Grandma shared, I also know that they were like sisters. They left Rozdół together and started a new life in Poland. They only split up because Josef gave his word that he would find Anita's relatives and sent a few letters to her aunts and uncles. When Anita's aunt replied, it was tough for my grandma to say goodbye to her. Anita did not want to leave them either to move abroad with a complete stranger, but all of them knew it would be a better life for her somewhere far away. A few years ago, when I visited Anita in Toronto, I brought her all the letters that she had written to Grandma during her life.*

*In 1998, my great-grandparents and grandmother were named as Righteous Among the Nations at a ceremony at the Israeli embassy in Warsaw. Their names appear in the Garden of the Righteous at Yad Vashem. This makes me and our whole family very proud. I took my parents there a few years ago, and all of us feel relief that people like them from around Europe will never be forgotten so that new generations will be able to learn that lesson.*

*I was proud to represent my family and stand together with Anita at last year's March of the Living ceremony. Since my Grandma passed away, Anita has become like a grandmother to me, and I am very proud to be considered her granddaughter. It is amazing and very inspiring to have her in my life.*

# Branching Out

Despite not earning a teaching degree, I went on to teach thousands of students about the Holocaust for more than three decades. It took me a long time to be able to speak about my wartime experiences. The two trials (in 1985 and 1988) of Holocaust denier Ernst Zündel and the rise of Holocaust denial around the world motivated many survivors, me included, to speak up. I thought that perhaps it was my duty to do something about it. There were not that many survivors, even then; most were old, and they were dying out. I believe it's important that we leave testimonies, that we bear witness — as Elie Wiesel famously said, "For the dead and the living, we must bear witness." It was very painful to hear people say that the Holocaust never happened, when I was there, when I and so many others lived through it. I mean, if the Holocaust never took place, then what happened to those six million Jews? Where are my parents? Where were all the people if they didn't die, as Zündel claimed?

In many ways, I have my great-uncle Chaim (Joachim) Schoenfeld to thank for motivating me to speak openly about my wartime experiences. At the age of ninety, Uncle Chaim wrote and self-published two important books about Polish Jewry and the Holocaust: *Holocaust Memoirs: Jews in the Lwow Ghetto, the Janowski Concentration Camp, and Deportees in Siberia* (1985) and *Shtetl Memoirs: Jewish Life in Galicia under the Austro-Hungarian Empire and the Reborn Poland, 1898–1939* (1985).

My uncle Chaim survived the Janowska concentration camp, but sadly, his first wife, Ola (my paternal grandmother's sister), and his elder son were murdered by the Nazis. Chaim's younger son escaped German occupation and joined the Soviet army. He was lost during the war.

Uncle Chaim came into my life in the fall of 1957, a few months after Ricky was born. He and his new wife, Tatiana, had immigrated to Canada from Germany, where they had lived after leaving Poland. Chaim secured a job in Hamilton. A few months before their arrival, Chaim wrote to me, having received my address from my aunt Rachel in Israel. I do not know how he found Rachel. In this letter, Chaim introduced himself as my great-uncle. Chaim shared how he and Ola had helped my grandfather Moshe look after my infant father after my grandmother died in childbirth. He knew my father throughout his life.

When Chaim retired from his work in Hamilton, he and Tatiana moved to Toronto, and we had the opportunity to see them more often. We all cherished Uncle Chaim, and he was like a grandfather to my children. He held Peter at his *brit milah* and Ruthie's daughter Yaelle at her naming. Chaim passed away in 1995 at the age of a hundred.

Uncle Chaim used to visit local schools on behalf of the Holocaust Centre of Toronto's survivor speakers' program, talking to students about his Holocaust experiences, and I used to drive him. One day, my uncle and I were at a school when a student asked a question about surviving the Holocaust. Uncle Chaim pointed to me and said, "Ask her." Just like that! And that was the first time I spoke to students about my own experiences in the Holocaust.

After the Holocaust Centre of Toronto opened in 1985, I became involved in Holocaust education. Although it was and continues to be difficult for me to relive those war years, I began sharing my story with students through the Holocaust Centre's survivor speakers' bureau at schools and at the centre. The centre's name is now the

Sarah and Chaim Neuberger Holocaust Education Centre. Following a United Jewish Appeal trip to Israel in 1989, the head of the UJA requested that I chair the Holocaust Centre, a position I held for one year. That first year I was chair, I assumed responsibility for organizing a very successful survivor speakers series. I was also involved in presenting the *We Were Children Just Like You* photograph exhibit (with Yaffa Eliach) and was appointed chair of a major international Anne Frank exhibit that was presented at the Canadian National Exhibition (CNE) in Toronto. I was honoured to speak at both events. Thirty years later, I am still involved at the Neuberger as an educator.

I also joined the Holocaust Resource Program committee at Baycrest. Founded and coordinated by the centre's former senior social worker Dr. Paula David, the committee was dedicated to helping elderly survivor residents and educating staff to better understand the survivors' behaviours, such as a refusal to take a shower or line up. The committee provided education around identifying triggers that frightened the survivors and brought up memories of their experiences in the camps. Paula David was instrumental in writing and publishing a book on the topic, *Caring for Aging Holocaust Survivors: A Practice Manual*. Paula also started a child survivor support group, which some of the residents joined. The groups were very small, and with Paula's help, the members managed to resolve some of their problems. Paula David now teaches at the Ontario Institute for Studies in Education (OISE) at the University of Toronto, and Shoshana Jacobi continues to run the small groups at Baycrest today.

Frank didn't think it was good for me to relive my experiences. I, on the other hand, needed to get them out and express them. Frank accompanied me to an early gathering of Holocaust survivors in Washington, D.C. In the main meeting space, there was a wall of notices — survivors seeking lost friends and relatives. I went over and added my own note to inquire if anybody had known my parents, Fisko and Edzia Helfgott.

Suddenly, all these reporters swarmed me, wanting to interview me, and Frank told them, "No, not now." That night at the hotel we had the worst fight of our lives. I said to him, "You don't let me talk. And it's all sitting in here, in my heart and my head. I won't get hurt, and maybe it will be better to get it out." Frank thought he was protecting me; he believed that keeping my Holocaust story within the family would shield me from reliving the trauma. I could appreciate that any concerns he had were out of love. But I was so angry! This was my story; why couldn't I talk?

After that night, Frank was never anything but extremely supportive of my work as a survivor educator. I think it made me feel saner and more fulfilled, as if I was doing something that was important. It also helped me cope with some of my pain. In fact, Frank became so supportive of my activities and of Holocaust education in general that he surprised me by establishing a special collection at the Holocaust Centre of Toronto in my name: the Anita Ekstein Holocaust Resource Collection. I recently added Frank's name to the library. The Frank and Anita Ekstein Collection includes almost nine thousand books, oral and written testimonies, films and other materials for teaching about the Holocaust. It is a terribly important place to me, a beautiful gift and a true testament to Frank's love for me.

Through my volunteer work at the Holocaust Centre, I met other survivors, but not necessarily child survivors or hidden children. They were mostly camp survivors, like my aunt and her survivor friends, who were much older than me. To the best of my knowledge, I did not meet another child survivor until 1991. Everything changed when I met Eve Bergstein. Before we met, Eve played a central role in establishing a speakers' bureau and annual Holocaust symposium for high school students in Kitchener, Ontario. When she was working to introduce a project to interview local Holocaust survivors, she turned to the Holocaust Centre of Toronto for help. They shared my video testimony to demonstrate how the interviews were conducted.

As Eve watched the footage, she thought, "Oh my God! This is my story." She had also been hidden by Polish people during the war.

Eve phoned me, and the two of us met at Diana Sweets in Yorkdale Shopping Centre. We sat for four hours, talking and crying. Eve was the first person I met who had similar experiences to mine. The crazy thing is that we had both attended Humewood Public School in Toronto at the same time. It's a wonder we hadn't met sooner. Somehow, nobody ever thought to introduce the two Jewish immigrant orphans to each other!

Once we became friends, I supported Eve's annual symposium by bringing Toronto-based Holocaust survivors to speak at the program. Since this time, we have both lost our husbands and see each other regularly in Toronto and in Florida, where she rents an apartment close to me.

A turning point in my life came when Eve Bergstein and I attended the first Hidden Children Conference in New York City in 1991. Until then, it hadn't dawned on me that child survivors like myself could have real memories of our Holocaust experiences! Before that, all we heard was, "What do you know? You weren't in the camps." That's what Aunt Sally used to say, and it was the message echoed by all of her survivor friends. I realize now how difficult it must have been for her to see me alive with her own two kids gone. She was good to me, but she wasn't well because of her time in the camps, and she could not appreciate that I had lost my parents and had also suffered.

With the 1991 conference, the status of hidden children was finally legitimized. When I returned home to Toronto, I started a group for child survivors and hidden children. I had not known other hidden children before meeting Eve, and I did not know if there were others in Toronto. I placed an advertisement in the *Canadian Jewish News*, and I was shocked when seventy-five people came to our first meeting. We came together to talk and comfort each other; we shared our memories and our pain and our losses. We had not been allowed to be children or experience a normal childhood, and somehow, we became adults. We could never know what our lives might have been like with parents, with family, with roots. We shared our stories, our history, and everyone could empathize, regardless of which country in Europe we came from. It was good to be with peers who understood. Our group has been together now for twenty-eight years, and we have created a community of sisters and brothers, the family that we were denied because of the Holocaust. We have lost many members since 1991. Now we just meet socially, four times a year, often in conjunction with holidays. And, it is always all about food! Today, I finally have a co-chair, a Dutch child survivor named Leonard Vis, to share responsibilities with.

With the support of the UJA, Eve Bergstein and I organized the International Conference of Jewish Child Survivors of the Holocaust and Second Generation in Toronto in 2002. It took two years of work, but we were rewarded with a very successful event involving five hundred attendees from around the world. Our keynote speakers included Rosalie Abella, the first Jewish woman to sit on the Supreme Court of Canada, and Dr. Robert Krell, a psychiatrist and hidden child from the Netherlands. It was a deeply meaningful event for all of those involved, and worth the effort.

Presently, I am a member of the advisory committee of the Neuberger Holocaust Education Centre, and I remain actively involved as one of the centre's survivor speakers, addressing students of all denominations. As a Holocaust educator, I have travelled to local as well as more distant schools to address large groups of students. I regularly speak with classes in Kitchener, Waterloo and Cambridge, Ontario. Survivor educators are treated like gold: we are transported to and from the schools in a limousine, and the teachers are simply incredible. Meeting us is a huge deal for the students we engage with, as it is unlikely they have ever met a Holocaust survivor before or will ever meet one again. Each year there are fewer and fewer of us; soon there will no longer be any eyewitnesses to the Nazi atrocities. The world will then need to rely on evidence, our testimonies and our descendants to keep our stories alive.

I am lucky that my children know about their family history, and that all of them have accompanied me on trips back to Poland. I feel that it is my responsibility to teach younger people about the Holocaust for as long as I can, although I do not speak as much as I used to. It really takes everything out of me. But when we're together, I introduce students to lost members of my family, keeping their memories alive, as well as the life that existed before the Nazis entered our hometown. With great sensitivity but brutal honesty, I describe the immense hatred and antisemitism that led to the destruction of one thousand years of Jewish life in Poland and to the murder of six million European Jews, 1.5 million of them innocent children. The impact of these numbers on the students is clear; it is reflected in their respect and appreciation for me and in their questions.

My contributions to Holocaust education were never limited to the Toronto area or the Neuberger Holocaust Education Centre. In 1996, I went on the March of the Living for the first time with several dozen Canadian teenagers. I continued participating in the March in 1998, 2000 and 2001. Every year I came home with bronchitis because I was not sleeping well, and the trips were very emotionally and physically draining for me. Frank saw that it was hard for me to go on these trips and asked me not to go again. And he also did not like being alone for two weeks! After going on the March three times, I took a break until 2004.

In 2005, I went to Bełżec with the March of the Living, and in the museum there I saw that a transport had arrived from Stryj on October 18, 1942, the day my mother was taken from the ghetto. There is no way of knowing if my mother died in transit or in the gas chambers, so I mark the date of her death as October 18. I have visited Bełżec many times with the March of the Living; my children Ruth and Peter have accompanied me to Bełżec, as well as six of my grandchildren. The visit was understandably emotional and memorable for all of us. I still feel so lucky to have escaped the same fate as my mother by minutes. Until a memorial to the victims and a small museum were erected in 2004, the former camp site was a dump littered with garbage and communist propaganda. It was a terrible place. Now, there are two concrete slabs at the memorial, one listing names of women who were victims and the other for men. My mother's name — Edzia, or Ettel in Yiddish — is inscribed on the monument. I say Kaddish every time I visit.

In 2006, I was appointed national chair of March of the Living Canada, where I served for three years and worked closely with the program's director, Eli Rubenstein. Since 2004, the only year I have not participated was 2009, when the trip overlapped with my granddaughter Stephanie's wedding. My children Ruth and Peter, and my niece Dori, have all accompanied me on the trip as chaperones.

We spend the first week of every trip in Poland, followed by a second week in Israel. Before leaving for Poland, I would speak to the kids at eight seminars and at a Shabbaton. This is when I would meet the participants and tell them my story for the first time. In Poland, I served as an eyewitness, sharing my perspective, which differed from that of the educators and the chaperones. This is a critical learning opportunity for the teenagers. We who were children during the Holocaust are the last surviving witnesses. We have memories, and our memories are unique, though very fragile and very painful. Everywhere we go there are always questions about my personal Holocaust story, the history of Polish Jews before the war, and, of course, about how anyone — let alone an entire people — could possibly overcome the kinds of atrocities that the Nazis inflicted on the Jews. When the March moves on to Israel, everyone is ready for a celebration of life and renewal. And by the time I get back to Canada I need a long break.

In Poland, the March includes a visit to the town of Tykocin, where a pogrom occurred in 1941. On August 25–26, 1941, the town's entire Jewish community — over 1,400 men, women and children — were marched to the nearby Łopuchowo forest and murdered by the Einsatzgruppen, and their bodies were dumped into three mass graves. We don't tell the kids where they are going. It's always very quiet on the bus, and there is a long walk into the forest from the road, so I think they already have an idea where they are headed. They understand that they are following the same route taken by the Jews of Tykocin. Absolute silence! The birds are singing, and I'm thinking, they must have been singing at the time of the pogrom, too. It is a horrible place. And then, of course, the kids see where they are. In an instance, the kids go from believing they know everything to seeing a site like this. There is a complete change in them, and the adults are always there to support them.

The Auschwitz-Birkenau Memorial and Museum also has a profound effect on them. It's like nothing they have ever experienced before. There's one building in particular that always stresses me out: the one featuring a wall of hair that belonged to Jews and other victims who were deported to the camp. The teenage girls take one look at the wall, and they really freak out. On one of my trips there were so many gorgeous girls with long, luxurious hair. I took one look at the girls and at the wall of hair, and I was done. I couldn't help it — I completely fell apart thinking that this hair belonged to kids just like them. There are always emotional triggers, but I'm getting older, and it's becoming harder.

It's not easy for any of us, and I thought about stopping these trips for a while before I did. But then I would think of all the kids that I'd helped educate about the Holocaust over the years. I meet them all over the place. I remember their faces, but I don't know their names. They always remind me that we met and share stories about our time together. And this is exactly why I participated on the March for so many years. Eli Rubenstein, the national director of March of the Living Canada, recalls the March of the Living in 2008, when I stood in front of thousands of young people from around the world who were marching from Auschwitz to Birkenau on Holocaust Remembrance Day and told my daughter Ruth, "You see? Hitler did not win." He also recalls one speech I gave in a shaky voice, pleading with the students: "We can't continue to hate forever. It has to end somewhere."

My grandson Leor gave a speech addressing me while we were at Bełżec in 2010. The following is an excerpt from it:

*Grandma, you have not only had a major impact on my life, but also on all my friends and every Jew and non-Jew you have ever told your story to.*

*Grandma, there are many survivors of the Holocaust that decided to live their lives happily and not share their experiences with their family or anyone at all. Not only have you shared your story and life experiences with us, but you made it your life mission to teach and educate people from all around the world about your horrible experiences, and you have touched each and every one of us deeply....*

March of the Living has grown a lot since my first trip back in 1996. Twenty years later, in 2016, there were six buses of students on the March from Toronto alone. Some 60 per cent of the kids were students at CHAT (the Community Hebrew Academy of Toronto). There was also one bus of university students and young professionals, and two buses of adults. In total, between twelve and thirteen thousand March of the Living participants from around the world came together for this special program. What a wonderful feeling!

All but two of my grandchildren have participated in the program. On the one hand, it was important to have my grandkids there with me. But on the other hand, it bothered me that they had to witness the impact of Nazi atrocities, especially the Bełżec death camp. My children and grandchildren know that my mother and her family and many other members of my extended family were murdered there. It's devastating for me that my grandchildren need to experience these tragic memories with me. Three of my great-nieces, Jessica, Jordana and Danielle, and a great-nephew, Evan, have also participated on the March of the Living program with me.

In 2016, my friend Nate Leipciger and I participated in our sixteenth trip together. This time, before we even got home, he asked me, "Nu, are we going next year?" And I said, "You're crazy. Don't ask me now." He was eighty-eight years old. It's good to be such an optimist. I don't know where he finds that kind of energy. But I did go with him again, on two more trips.

Over the years I have received many honours for my volunteering and contributions to Holocaust education. In September 1986, I was the first recipient of the Coordinated Services to the Jewish Elderly (later called Circle of Care) Marie and Jack Freedman Memorial Award in recognition of my volunteer work with seniors. I was awarded the UJA's Shem Tov Award in 1991, followed by a certificate of recognition from the Government of Ontario on April 12, 1995, granted by The Honourable Bob Rae, then Premier of Ontario. In 1998, I received the Yad Vashem award for contributions to Holocaust education, and in 2001, I was honoured with the Elie Wiesel Holocaust Remembrance Medal.

Among the other honours I have received are a certificate of recognition from the Government of Ontario for service to Holocaust education, bestowed by the Honourable Mike Colle, then minister of citizenship and immigration (2006); the Canadian Society for Yad Vashem Award (2009); Ve'ahavta Tikun Olam Humanitarian Award (2009); and the Israel Bonds Golda Meir Leadership Award (2012). In addition, on September 27, 2000, two representatives of the Canadian House of Commons — Deputy Prime Minister Herb Gray and Hedy Fry, the secretary of state for Multiculturalism and Status of Women — held a ceremony to mark the fifty-fifth anniversary of liberation of Nazi oppression. I was nominated to participate in the moving ceremony, where I received an award for my contributions to Canadian society. All three of my children were in attendance.

I am obviously deeply honoured and moved by these tributes. Imagine: all this for a little orphaned survivor who immigrated from Poland! It is gratifying to know that all my hard work has made a difference. But, believe me, all the awards mean nothing compared to the satisfaction I get when I teach kids about the Holocaust and join my grandchildren on the March of the Living.

# Epilogue

Frank and I did not take any holidays when the kids were little: it was difficult with small children, and we had no money. The first vacation we took was in November 1963, after nearly nine years of marriage. We hired a woman to take care of the children, and we went to Florida for one week with our friends Ethel and Harold Landis, and Frank's cousins Richard and Doris Popper. The holiday was wonderful, but it was late fall and the weather was not great. We sat on the beach covered with towels to keep warm and laughed. I remember that when we landed in Toronto, we were told that President Kennedy had been assassinated in Dallas.

Once we became more established, Frank and I travelled to Israel for the first time in 1972. I had wanted to see my aunt Rachel whom I last saw when I was a child. It was a very emotional reunion. Aside from me, my father's half-sister Rachel was the only Helfgott to survive the Holocaust in Europe. Before the German occupation, Rachel was married to a man whose last name was Strupp, and she worked as a teacher in Poland. Rachel survived the war on false papers, hidden in barns and forests. Sadly, she lost her husband and a nine-month-old baby in the Holocaust. After the war, Rachel made it out of Soviet-occupied Poland on a boat destined for pre-state Israel. After detainment in Cyprus, Rachel eventually settled on Kibbutz Afek, where she worked as a teacher. Rachel married Josef Shafrir, and they had two daughters, Yonat and Shoshana, who still live in Israel. My aunt Rachel died in Israel in 2006. It is thanks to her that I know so much about my father.

During that same visit, we met my aunt Elsa who had immigrated from the Belgian Congo. Sadly, she died of cancer before we could go to Israel again.

In 1976, Frank and I brought the kids along on our second visit to Israel. It was a marvellous vacation. They had the chance to meet their cousins, explore the sites, and develop a connection to Israel. The visit was especially important to Peter: after graduating from high school in January 1980, he went to Israel and spent a few months on Kibbutz Yagur, near Haifa. He made lifelong friends there, and we had a difficult time getting him to come home. Peter eventually returned to Toronto to attend Rick's wedding to Lillian Wlosko, on August 10, 1980, and to attend York University.

Peter's love of Israel continues until today, and he travels there several times a year. He speaks Hebrew fluently and is deeply committed to several causes, among them the OneFamily Fund for victims of terror and their families, based in Israel. He is a past board member of the UJA and was instrumental in founding C-CAT, the Canadian Coalition Against Terror. For his efforts he was awarded the Queen Elizabeth II Silver Jubilee Medal. Peter married Stella Amar on June 9, 1985, and they are parents to Eli, Orli and Leor.

Ruth and Rick are also engaged in various community initiatives. In many ways Ruth followed in my footsteps. Ruth attended McMaster University with plans to enter medicine but found her calling as an occupational therapist. After working for many years, she retired and now volunteers her time as a docent for the Neuberger Holocaust Centre. She has served as the chair of Women's Philanthropy for the United Jewish Appeal and never ceases to amaze me. Ruthie married Alan Lechem on May 8, 1988, and gave us Cobi, Lara and Yaelle.

Rick graduated from York University and joined the family business, Weston Road Lumber (now known as Weston Forest Group) in

1978. By this time, Frank had gradually bought out shares in the business and assumed control of the company. Under the management of Frank, Rick, and later Peter and Alan, Weston flourished. The company grew from a single lumber yard with twelve employees into the Weston Forest Group, one of the largest and most diverse wholesalers, distributors and remanufacturers of forest products in Canada. One of Canada's foremost lumber product companies, it conducted business on four continents and in more than forty countries in its heyday. Weston has repeatedly been named as one of "Canada's Best Managed Companies." Rick, Peter and Alan still run Weston enterprises today.

Outside of work, Rick is politically active and a major supporter of the Conservative Party of Canada. He is interested in political issues affecting all aspects of society and is committed to improving the quality of life for all Canadians. Rick and Lillian are parents to my eldest grandchildren, Stephanie and Michelle. Frank and I were thrilled that all of our children found life partners and blessed us with beautiful grandchildren whom we have loved and enjoyed. I am so proud of my children for their philanthropic natures and volunteer work, as well as their love of Judaism and Canada. Like me, they are comfortable and proud of being Jewish in a free Canada. I am also proud of my niece-in-law, Dori Ekstein, with whom I have a very close relationship. She, like Ruth, devotes her time and energy to Holocaust education. Dori has even received an award for chairing Holocaust Education Week three years in a row!

Despite numerous household and volunteer obligations, Frank and I always made time for his parents, Aunt Sally and Uncle Jack, Uncle Chaim Schoenfeld and Tatiana, and our good friends. Frank's father, Ernest, passed away in 1973; my mother-in-law, Anna, lived until 2001. Uncle Jack had a heart condition, like his two brothers, and he died suddenly from a heart attack in November 1980. Aunt Sally could not be alone after this loss and moved into Baycrest, where I assumed sole responsibility for her. Although Aunt Sally got better after Jack died, she was generally a difficult and unhappy person. It was not easy, to say the least. She died in 1994 at the age of ninety-two. They are all dearly missed.

My cousins Stefan and Zygmunt, who immigrated to Venezuela with their families after the war, are now deceased. Ania and Luis, Stefan's wife and son, left Venezuela for Spain several years ago to escape a volatile political situation. We are still in touch. Zygmunt's wife, Lucia, is now in her mid-nineties. She lives in Venezuela and is cared for by her elder daughter, Bogusia, who is a doctor. I have written to them on a number of occasions: "The warning signs are there. We've learned our lesson. Get out while you can." I'm afraid that one day they will be trapped. Zygmunt and Lucia's second daughter, Ania, is married to Ryszard Horowitz. Ryszard, his sister and parents were also saved by Oskar Schindler. Ania is now retired from a long career as an architect with the United Nations. She and Ryszard live in New York and have two sons.

Bogusia's daughter, Lotty, and her husband saw the signs that things were going to get worse and left Venezuela. The couple waited twelve years to get a green card and now live in Miami, Florida, with their three sons. We see each other when I am in Florida. Bogusia's son Leo and his family remain in Venezuela. I am very worried for their safety.

Frank and I moved to our dream house, with a pool, at 464 Woodland Acres Crescent in 1990. We spent some wonderful times there with our children, grandchildren and friends. In the winters, Frank and I and friends, fourteen of us in total, would go to Aruba. We had great times together. Frank and I also did quite a lot of travelling. We visited Israel yearly, and travelled through most of Europe, Australia, New Zealand and China. We also took some cruises to Alaska and in 2001 sailed from Copenhagen to the Scandinavian countries and Saint Petersburg, Russia.

The two of us had a good life and a good marriage. There were days of great fun and days of irritation and hurt. But through it all was love. A quote from the French actress Simone Signoret sums up our marriage perfectly: "Chains do not hold a marriage together. It is thread, hundreds of tiny threads which sew people together through the years."

In the early winter of 2003, Frank and I rented an apartment in Florida to see if we would like it there. We decided to buy an apartment and made plans to move there the following year. Furniture and accessories were purchased, and we looked forward to spending many winters there. It was not to be.

~

On April 20, 2003, Frank was in a terrible car accident. He never regained consciousness, and I could not say goodbye. After two horrible weeks, we lost him on May 5, 2003. We were all devastated. I have no words to describe what it was like for me — part of me died with him. I did not know how I would survive without him. The physical and mental pain was so horrific, I had difficulty breathing. I could not sleep. For the second time in my life I was alone and afraid. I had loved him with all my heart. In his arms, I felt secure and loved; no matter what was troubling me, Frank always made it better. His death affected me greatly. Until you lose the love of your life, your lover and partner with whom you spent fifty-one years of your life, forty-eight years of them married, it is impossible to understand. I do not wish this pain on anyone.

It seemed like history was repeating itself. I could not say goodbye to my mother, and now I missed a goodbye with Frank. I had a very difficult time for months, during which I relived those terrible war years.

Frank has now been gone for sixteen years. Based on the amount of pain in my heart and the tears I still shed today, you would think he died just a few months ago. I miss Frank terribly even though he has been gone for many years. Life alone is difficult and very lonely. After fifty-one years, I had to learn to be alone again.

Before Frank's untimely passing, we had purchased a pre-construction condo in Toronto. When it was ready, I sold our house and moved to the condo, on December 1, 2004. Leaving our dream house was very hard for me. We had such good times there and made beautiful memories.

The condo we bought in Florida was also closed after Frank's death. My son Ricky dealt with this. I wanted to get rid of it and could not imagine living there without Frank. But the sellers had already bought a house, and their lawyer threatened to sue if we reneged on the deal. Ricky said, "Try it mom, if you don't like it, we will sell it." So I went to stay there in December 2004 for the first time. Peter came with me for a few days and helped me get set up. I made friends, learned to play bridge, read a lot, took some courses and time passed. Every year it is easier to be there.

For many years, I was involved in volunteer work. After Frank's death, I had to keep busy — it kept me sane. I returned to my volunteer groups and committees with a newfound strength and purpose. To know I had somewhere to go and something to do got me out of the apartment. I started to travel again: to South Africa, Italy and Sicily with people from my condo. Later, I went with the Canadian Friends of Hebrew University group to Lithuania, Latvia, Greece and Israel. I also took several river cruises in France and Russia.

I was away on a river cruise to the beaches in Normandy when I got news of my son Peter's accident in July 2015. He was jogging near his cottage when he was hit by a pickup truck. God must have been with us. Despite having serious injuries and a very difficult recovery, by some miracle he is doing well.

In July 2014, my children and grandchildren made me a beautiful party for my eightieth birthday. All my cousins came: Michael and Marcia, Steven and Beth and Elaine and Stanley from New York, Jeffrey and Cathy from Atlanta, and Darryl from Saint Louis. Terry and Michael flew in from Minneapolis. My friends, some from my

Central Commerce days and others whom I was fortunate to meet later, all came. It was a wonderful party!

After Frank's death, I also resumed going on the March of the Living. In 2017, my seventeenth trip, my granddaughter Michelle went with me as a chaperone. She missed going as a teenager when her trip was cancelled because of the intifada in Israel. Michelle said to me, "Grandma, I need you to go with me," and I made it happen. She was the seventh of my grandchildren to go on the March with me. I have loved having them with me. I have two great-nephews who haven't gone yet. Hopefully they'll still go and know that I'm there with them in spirit. And that they can come home and hug me and we will cry together.

In 2018, I went on my eighteenth and last trip. The trips were mentally and physically challenging, but it brought me great satisfaction to travel with and teach intelligent, curious and compassionate teenagers. They showed me tremendous respect and appreciation, and I tried to do the same for them.

Over the last decade I spoke more frequently at the Holocaust Centre and in schools than ever before. I made sure I had something to do every day and kept busy so that I could sleep at night. My children and grandchildren have been supportive every step of the way. Seven years ago, Stephanie and her husband, Michael Shapiro, gave me a great-granddaughter, Emily Joelle, and two years ago, another great-granddaughter, Hallie. I have tried to instill in my family the meaning and pride of being Jewish. I have told them about my parents and what they stood for. We have all been to Israel, where we took in the exhibitions at Yad Vashem together. I have taught my family to love, not hate.

The Holocaust was a dreadful time in the history of humankind, not only for the Jews but for all people. Human beings allowed this to happen; they stood by and watched the destruction. If people allowed it to happen once, they just may allow it to happen again. And if not to Jews, then to some other people. I am not sure we've learned our lesson, but I certainly hope so.

I still have nightmares occasionally and wake up in a cold sweat, believing I am being hunted by the Germans. The memories seem to become more vivid as I've aged. I cannot imagine they will ever disappear. I often wonder: Would I have the courage to save a stranger from imminent death? I certainly hope so. My rescuers absolutely knew the gamble they were taking in hiding me. And yet the more I think about what it took to survive those terrible years, the more I realize how miraculous it was that I beat the odds. Whenever I look at my beautiful great-granddaughters, Emily and Hallie, I am reminded of this miracle. How did we make it to four generations? I wasn't supposed to survive. Everything I hold dear to me — my family, friends and community — came about because of one wonderful, righteous man who had the courage to save a little Jewish girl. He will always be in my heart.

# Glossary

**Aktion** (German; pl. *Aktionen*) A brutal roundup of Jews for mass murder by shooting or for deportation to forced labour, concentration and death camps.

**antisemitism** Prejudice, discrimination, persecution or hatred against Jewish people, institutions, culture and symbols.

**"Aryan"** A nineteenth-century anthropological term originally used to refer to the Indo-European family of languages and, by extension, the peoples who spoke them. It became a synonym for people of Nordic or Germanic descent in the theories that inspired Nazi racial ideology. "Aryan" was an official classification in Nazi racial laws to denote someone of pure Germanic blood, as opposed to "non-Aryans," such as Slavs, Jews, part-Jews, Roma and Sinti, and others of supposedly inferior racial stock.

**"Aryanization"/ "Aryanize"** The process of transferring businesses owned by Jews to non-Jews, or "Aryans," who were considered racially superior. From 1933 to 1938 in Nazi Germany, Jewish business owners were compelled to sell their devalued businesses to non-Jews at radically low prices, and in 1938, new regulations required Jews to transfer their businesses to non-Jews for almost no compensation. In other countries in occupied Europe, "Aryanization" laws were introduced to expropriate Jewish property and were implemented by governments that collaborated with the Nazis, such as Vichy France.

**Auschwitz** (German; in Polish, Oświęcim) A Nazi concentration camp complex in German-occupied Poland about 50 kilometres from Krakow, on the outskirts of the town of Oświęcim, built between 1940 and 1942. The largest camp complex established by the Nazis, Auschwitz contained three main camps: Auschwitz I, a concentration camp; Auschwitz II (Birkenau), a death camp that used gas chambers to commit mass murder; and Auschwitz III (also called Monowitz or Buna), which provided slave labour for an industrial complex. In 1942, the Nazis began to deport Jews from almost every country in Europe to Auschwitz, where they were selected for slave labour or for death in the gas chambers. In mid-January 1945, close to 60,000 inmates were sent on a death march, leaving behind only a few thousand inmates who were liberated by the Soviet army on January 27, 1945. It is estimated that 1.1 million people were killed in Auschwitz, approximately 90 per cent of whom were Jewish; other victims included Polish prisoners, Roma and Soviet prisoners of war. *See also* Birkenau.

**babushka** (Russian; grandmother) An old Russian woman.

**Bandera, Stepan** (1909–1959) A leader of a Ukrainian nationalist movement, the Organization of Ukrainian Nationalists (OUN), and head of its terrorist activities and military wing. Bandera collaborated with the Nazis in the hope they would help establish an independent Ukraine that was cleansed of its ethnic enemies: Poles, Soviets and Jews. His followers, known as Banderites (Banderowcy), were responsible for the massacre of tens of thousands of Jews and Poles during World War II. After Bandera declared an independent Ukrainian state in 1941, the Nazis arrested him and then deported him to Sachsenhausen concentration camp. Bandera was released in 1944 and continued to lead the OUN and collaborate with the Nazis. He was assassinated by the KGB in 1959. In recent years, Bandera has gained popularity among Ukrainian nationalists as a symbol of freedom and independence. *See also* Banderowcy.

**Banderowcy** (Polish) Bands of Ukrainian nationalists who killed

Jews and Poles during the Holocaust with the goal of creating an ethnically pure, independent Ukraine. Led by Stepan Bandera of the Organization of Ukrainian Nationalists (OUN) and linked to its military wing, the Ukrainian Insurgent Army (UPA), the Banderowcy used the German occupation to pursue its own program of killing. *See also* Bandera, Stepan.

**baptism** A religious ritual symbolizing acceptance into the Christian church. The ritual involves immersion in water or sprinkling a few drops of water on the forehead.

**Baron de Hirsch farming project / fund** A fund established by the wealthy German Jewish philanthropist Baron Maurice de Hirsch (1831–1896) to provide resettlement assistance to Jewish immigrants who were facing poverty and persecution in Eastern Europe. Believing that Jews could best support themselves by farming, Hirsch established the Jewish Colonization Association, which set up agricultural settlements for Jewish immigrants in Canada, the United States, Argentina, Brazil and Palestine.

**Bełżec** A Nazi killing centre established in 1942 in the Lublin district of German-occupied Poland. Bełżec was the first of three death camps built specifically for the implementation of Operation Reinhard, the planned mass murder of the Jews in occupied Poland. Arrivals to the camp were immediately led to gas chambers that were labelled as showers, where they were gassed with carbon monoxide. Between March and December 1942, approximately 450,000 Jews were murdered in Bełżec, as well as an unknown number of Roma and Poles.

**Birkenau** Also known as Auschwitz II. One of the camps in the Auschwitz complex in German-occupied Poland and the largest death camp established by the Nazis. Birkenau was built in 1941, and in 1942 the Nazis designated it as a killing centre, using Zyklon B gas to carry out the systematic murder of Jews and other people considered "undesirable" by the Nazis. In 1943, the Nazis began to use four crematoria with gas chambers that could hold up to 2,000 people each to murder the large numbers of Jews who were being brought to the camp from across Europe. Upon arrival, prisoners were selected for slave labour or sent to the gas chambers. The camp was liberated in January 1945 by the Soviet army. Approximately 1.1 million people were killed in the Auschwitz camp complex, most of them in Birkenau and the vast majority of them Jews. *See also* Auschwitz.

**blue laws** Laws that restrict secular activities, such as conducting business or providing public entertainment, on Sundays to enforce a day of rest. In Canada, the Lord's Day Act, which was instituted in 1906, prohibited businesses from operating on Sundays until it was declared unconstitutional in 1985.

**B'nai Brith** An international Jewish organization founded in New York in 1843 to combat antisemitism, strengthen Jewish identity, support communities and advocate for Israel and for Jews all over the world. The Canadian arm, founded in 1875, is headquartered in Toronto, with branches in other cities.

*brit milah* (Hebrew; in Yiddish, bris; covenant of circumcision) Judaism's religious ceremony to welcome male infants into the covenant between God and the Children of Israel through a ritual circumcision (removal of the foreskin of the penis) performed by a mohel, or circumciser, eight days after the baby is born. Traditionally, a baby boy is named at this ceremony.

**Brünnlitz** A Nazi labour camp on the site of Oskar Schindler's armaments factory complex located outside the town of Brněnec in Moravia, established in 1944. The camp was opened when Schindler learned that the Jewish labour force in his factory in Krakow was going to be sent to their deaths at Auschwitz-Birkenau, and he bribed the SS to allow him to save 1,000 Jews on the pretext that he needed them to work for the war effort. Brünnlitz was liberated by the Soviet army at the end of the war.

**Communion** (also Holy Communion, Eucharist) A Christian ceremony in which bread and wine are consecrated and consumed.

Some Christian traditions have a First Communion ceremony, which is a rite of passage for children aged seven or eight.

**The Conference on Jewish Material Claims Against Germany** A program set in motion in 1952 with the Reparations Agreement, signed between West Germany and Israel and requiring West Germany to pay Israel for the resettlement of Jewish refugees and to compensate individual Jews all over the world for property and livelihood lost because of Nazi persecution. Jews who were victims of the Holocaust receive compensation from Germany through the Conference on Jewish Material Claims Against Germany (Claims Conference), which negotiates with Germany to provide Holocaust survivors with social services, to recover property and assets and to fund Holocaust education and research. The Claims Conference distributes hundreds of millions of dollars annually to tens of thousands of Holocaust survivors around the world.

**confirmation** A religious ceremony in which a person becomes a full member of the Christian Church.

**displaced persons camps** Facilities set up by the Allied authorities and the United Nations Relief and Rehabilitation Administration (UNRRA) in October 1945 to resolve the refugee crisis that arose at the end of World War II. The camps provided temporary shelter and assistance to the millions of people — not only Jews — who had been displaced from their home countries as a result of the war and helped them prepare for resettlement.

**Einsatzgruppen** (German; task force) Units of Nazi SS and police that were charged with securing the territories occupied by Nazi Germany after the invasion of the Soviet Union in 1941. These mobile death squads, with the support of local collaborators, were responsible for rounding up and murdering over a million Jews and many others in mass shooting operations. They were a key component in the implementation of the Nazis' so-called Final Solution in Eastern Europe.

**Entebbe raid** Also known as Operation Entebbe or Operation

Thunderbolt. A hostage-rescue mission carried out by the Israel Defense Forces on July 3–4, 1976, at the Entebbe Airport in Uganda. On June 27, an Air France plane was hijacked by members of the Popular Front for the Liberation of Palestine and the German group the Revolutionary Cells and flown to Entebbe with the approval of the Ugandan government. The hijackers held 106 mostly Israeli or Jewish hostages in the airport, demanding the release of 53 Palestinian militants from prison. Over a hundred Israeli commandos were flown in from Israel and raided the Entebbe airport, rescuing 102 of the hostages in an operation that lasted ninety minutes.

**Four Questions** The questions that are recited at the start of the Passover seder, usually by the youngest child at the table. The questions revolve around the theme of how this night of commemoration of the Exodus from Egypt is different from other nights — e.g., Why do we eat unleavened bread? Why do we eat bitter herbs? The readings that follow answer the questions and in doing so tell the Exodus story. *See also* Passover.

*Generalgouvernement* (German; General Government) The area of central Poland that was occupied by Nazi Germany in September 1939. Made up of the districts of Warsaw, Krakow, Radom and Lublin, it was the area in which the Nazis carried out Operation Reinhard, their plan to kill the two million Jews living there using three killing centres established for that purpose in 1942.

**Gestapo** (German; abbreviation of Geheime Staatspolizei, the Secret State Police) The Nazi regime's brutal political police that operated without legal constraints to deal with its perceived enemies. The Gestapo was formed in 1933 under Hermann Göring; it was taken over by Heinrich Himmler in 1934 and became a department within the SS in 1939. During the Holocaust, the Gestapo set up offices in Nazi-occupied countries and was responsible for rounding up Jews and sending them to concentration and death camps. They also arrested, tortured and deported those who resisted Nazi policies. A number of Gestapo members also belonged to the Einsatzgruppen, the mobile killing squads responsible for mass shooting operations of Jews in the Soviet Union. In the camp system, Gestapo officials ran the Politische Abteilung (Political Department), which was responsible for prisoner registration, surveillance, investigation and interrogation. *See also* SS.

**greenie** A term, often derogatory, referring to someone who is inexperienced or new to a community.

**Gypsy** *See* Roma.

**Iron Curtain** A term made famous by former British prime minister Winston Churchill in 1946 that described the political and ideological barrier maintained by the Soviet Union to isolate its dependent allies in Eastern and Central Europe from non-Communist Western Europe after World War II. The Communist governments behind the Iron Curtain exerted rigid control over the flow of information and people to and from the West until the collapse of Communism in 1989.

**Jewish Immigrant Aid Society (JIAS)** An organization that has provided a variety of services to Jewish immigrants to Canada from 1919 to the present. Its origins trace back to the first assembly of the Canadian Jewish Congress in 1919 when it was faced with a Jewish refugee crisis in Canada after World War I. In 1955 the organization changed its name to Jewish Immigrant Aid Services of Canada.

**Kaddish** (Aramaic; holy. Also known as the Mourner's Kaddish or Mourner's Prayer.) The prayer recited by mourners at funerals and memorials and during Jewish prayer services. Kaddish is traditionally said by a relative of the deceased, for eleven months after the death of a parent and for thirty days after the death of a spouse or sibling, as well as each year on the anniversary of the death.

*kittel* (Yiddish; robe, coat) A white robe traditionally worn by men at Jewish High Holiday services and by bridegrooms at their weddings, and some Jews wear a *kittel* at the Passover seder. The white garment symbolizes purity and is sometimes used as a burial shroud.

**kosher** (Hebrew) Fit to eat according to Jewish dietary laws. Observant Jews follow a system of rules known as *kashruth* that regulates what can be eaten, how food is prepared and how animals are slaughtered. Food is kosher when it has been deemed fit for consumption according to this system of rules. There are several foods that are forbidden, most notably pork products and shellfish.

**March of the Living** An annual two-week program that takes place in Poland and Israel and aims to educate primarily Jewish students and young adults from around the world about the Holocaust and Jewish life before and during World War II. On Holocaust Memorial Day (Yom HaShoah), participants and Holocaust survivors march the three kilometres from Auschwitz to Birkenau to commemorate and honour all who perished in the Holocaust. Afterwards, participants travel to Israel and join in celebrations there for Israel's remembrance and independence days.

**Mass** The main religious service in the Roman Catholic Church during which a priest recites specific liturgy while wearing vestments, or ceremonial garments. The service commemorates Jesus, and the central act of Mass is the consecration of bread and wine, which is known as the Eucharist. Mass is traditionally offered on Sundays, as well as for the dead or on special occasions.

**matzah** (Hebrew; also matza, matzoh, matzot, matsah; in Yiddish, matze) The crisp flatbread made of flour and water that is eaten during the holiday of Passover, when eating leavened foods is forbidden. Matzah is eaten during the seder to commemorate the Israelites' slavery in Egypt and their redemption, when they left Egypt in haste and didn't have time to let their dough rise.

**mezuzah** (Hebrew; doorpost) The small piece of parchment containing the text of the central Jewish prayer, the Shema, which has been handwritten in ink by a scribe. Many Jews place this parchment on the doorposts of their homes, often in decorative cases.

**Midnight Mass** *See* Mass.

**Molotov-Ribbentrop Pact** (Also known as the German-Soviet Pact) The non-aggression treaty that was signed on August 23, 1939, and was colloquially known as the Molotov-Ribbentrop Pact after the names of its signatories, Soviet foreign minister Vyacheslav Molotov and German foreign minister Joachim von Ribbentrop. The main, public provision of the pact stipulated that the two countries would not go to war with each other for ten years and that they would both remain neutral if either one was attacked by a third party. A secret component of the arrangement was the division of Eastern Europe into Nazi and Soviet areas of occupation. The Nazis breached the pact by launching a major offensive against the Soviet Union on June 22, 1941.

**New Testament** The second of the two major volumes of the Christian Bible; it discusses the teachings of Jesus and the development of early Christianity. *See also* Old Testament.

**Old Testament** The first of the two major volumes of the Christian Bible; it is based on the Hebrew Bible (the Torah) and contains texts of law, history, prophecy and the wisdom literature of the ancient Israelites. *See also* New Testament.

**Orthodox** The religious practice of Jews for whom the observance of Judaism is rooted in the traditional rabbinical interpretations of the biblical commandments. Orthodox Jewish practice is characterized by strict observance of Jewish law and tradition, such as the prohibition to work on the Sabbath and certain dietary restrictions.

**Passover** (in Hebrew, Pesach) A Jewish festival that takes place in the spring and commemorates the exodus of the Israelite slaves from Egypt. The week-long festival begins with a lavish ritual meal called a seder, during which the story of the Exodus is told through the reading of a Jewish text called the Haggadah. During

Passover, Jews refrain from eating any leavened foods. The name of the festival refers to God's "passing over" the houses of the Jews and sparing their lives during the last of the ten plagues, when the first-born sons of Egyptians were killed by God. *See also* seder.

**Plaszow** A labour camp constructed by the Nazis in a suburb of Krakow in 1942 in an area that included two Jewish cemeteries. In January 1944, Plaszow became a concentration camp, and in September it reached its peak of over 20,000 inmates, many of whom had been transported there from camps further east. Inmates were used for slave labour in a stone quarry or textile factory and were subject to the volatile whims of camp commandant Amon Göth. It is estimated that between 30,000 to 50,000 Jewish, Polish and Roma prisoners went through the camp, and that 5,000 to 8,000 prisoners were killed there.

**pogrom** (Russian; to wreak havoc, to demolish) A violent attack on a distinct ethnic group, usually referring to deliberate attacks by mobs against Jews and Jewish property. The term came into common usage in the late nineteenth century after a wave of anti-Jewish riots swept through the Russian Empire.

**Red Army** (in Russian, *Krasnaya Armiya*) A term used from 1918 to 1946 for the Soviet Union's armed forces, which were founded when the Bolshevik Party came to power after the Russian Revolution. The original name was the Workers' and Peasants' Red Army, the colour red representing blood spilled while struggling against oppression.

**Righteous Among the Nations** A title given by Yad Vashem, the World Holocaust Remembrance Center in Jerusalem, to honour non-Jews who risked their lives to help save Jews during the Holocaust. A commission was established in 1963 to award the title. If a person fits certain criteria and the story is carefully checked, the honouree is awarded with a medal and certificate and is commemorated on the Wall of Honour at the Garden of the Righteous in Jerusalem.

**Roma** (singular male, Rom; singular female, Romni) A traditionally itinerant ethnic group originally from northern India and primarily located in Central and Eastern Europe. The Roma, who have been referred to pejoratively as Gypsies, have often lived on the fringes of society and been subject to persecution. During the Holocaust, which the Roma refer to as the *Porajmos* — the destruction or devouring — Roma were stripped of their citizenship under the Nuremberg Laws and were targeted for death under Hitler's race policies. It is estimated that between 220,000 and 500,000 Roma were murdered in the Holocaust. Roma Holocaust Memorial Day is commemorated on August 2. *See also* Gypsy.

**Rosh Hashanah** (Hebrew; New Year) The two-day autumn holiday that marks the beginning of the Jewish year and ushers in the High Holy Days. It is celebrated with a prayer service and the blowing of the *shofar* (ram's horn), as well as festive meals that include symbolic foods such as an apple dipped in honey, which symbolizes the desire for a sweet new year. *See also* Yom Kippur.

**Sambor ghetto** The area in the town of Sambor, Poland, in which the town's Jews were confined by the Nazis starting in March 1942. The ghetto held close to 6,500 Jews at first, and Jews from the surrounding areas were forced into the ghetto shortly after. A series of roundups began in the summer of 1942, and Jews were either selected for forced labour in the Janowska labour camp, murdered in Sambor or in the nearby Radłowice forest or deported to Bełżec or Majdanek. The last Jews in the ghetto were shot in the Radłowice forest in June 1943. Out of the 8,000 Jews who lived in Sambor before the war, only 160 survived. *See also* Bełżec.

**Schindler, Oskar** (1908–1974) The German-Czech businessman who saved the lives of more than 1,000 Jews, who are often referred to as *Schindlerjuden*, Schindler's Jews. Schindler, a member of the Nazi Party, took over a Jewish-owned enamel factory in 1939 and named it Deutsche Emailwarenfabrik, or Emalia. There, he employed Jewish workers from the nearby Krakow ghetto and then the forced labour camp of Plaszow, repeatedly intervening to preserve his workers' safety, often risking his life by advocating for them and bribing camp commandant Amon Göth and other Nazi officials. When the Plaszow camp was turned into a concentration camp in 1944, Schindler rescued more than 1,000 Jews from deportation to Auschwitz by declaring them to be essential to the war effort and transporting them to his new munitions factory in Brünnlitz, Moravia. Schindler was awarded the title of Righteous Among the Nations by Yad Vashem in 1993 and was the subject of Steven Spielberg's 1993 film *Schindler's List*, based on the novel *Schindler's Ark* by Thomas Keneally. *See also* Brünnlitz; Plaszow; Righteous Among the Nations.

**seder** (Hebrew; order) A ritual meal celebrated at the beginning of the festival of Passover. A traditional seder involves reading the Haggadah, which tells the story of the Israelite slaves' exodus from Egypt; drinking four cups of wine; eating matzah and other symbolic foods which are arranged on a special seder plate; partaking in a festive meal; and singing traditional songs. *See also* Four Questions; matzah; Passover.

**Shabbat** (Hebrew; in Yiddish, Shabbes, Shabbos) The weekly day of rest beginning Friday at sunset and ending Saturday at nightfall, ushered in by the lighting of candles on Friday evening and the recitation of blessings over wine and challah (egg bread). A day of celebration as well as prayer, it is customary to eat three festive meals, attend synagogue services and refrain from doing any work or travelling.

**Shabbaton** A weekend event focused on a communal celebration of Shabbat and other Jewish activities. *See also* Shabbat.

**shmata** (Yiddish) Rag.

**Siege of Leningrad** (also known as the 900-Day Siege) The siege of the city of Leningrad (St. Petersburg) in the Soviet Union by Nazi Germany starting on September 8, 1941, and lasting until January 27, 1944. The siege ended when a successful Soviet offensive drove the German forces from the city. The 872-day siege cut the city off from supplies, causing severe famine and disease and resulting in an estimated one million deaths, making it the deadliest siege in history.

**SS** (abbreviation of Schutzstaffel; Defence Corps) The elite police force of the Nazi regime that was responsible for security and for the enforcement of Nazi racial policies, including the implementation of the Final Solution — a euphemistic term referring to the Nazis' plan to systematically murder Europe's Jewish population. The SS was established in 1925 as Adolf Hitler's elite bodyguard unit, and under the direction of Heinrich Himmler, its membership grew from 280 in 1929 to 52,000 when the Nazis came to power in 1933, and to nearly a quarter of a million on the eve of World War II. SS recruits were screened for their racial purity and had to prove their "Aryan" lineage. The SS ran the concentration and death camps and also established the Waffen-SS, its own military division that was independent of the German army. *See also* Gestapo.

**Star of David** (in Hebrew, *Magen David*) The six-pointed star that is the most recognizable symbol of Judaism. During World War II, Jews in Nazi-occupied areas were frequently forced to wear a badge or armband with the Star of David on it as an identifying mark of their lesser status and to single them out as targets for persecution.

**The United Jewish Appeal (UJA)** A Jewish fundraising organization created in 1939 in response to persecution of Jews in Germany to provide support to Jewish communities in Europe, to bolster immigration to Palestine and to assist Jewish refugees in the United States. After World War II, the UJA supported Jews in displaced persons (DP) camps and helped them settle in Israel. The organization continues to provide financial support to Jewish communities throughout the world. The UJA is now part of the Jewish Federations of North America.

**Warsaw Ghetto Uprising** A large rebellion by Jewish resistance fighters in the Warsaw ghetto, beginning on April 19, 1943, and lasting several weeks. After the mass deportation and murder of ghetto inhabitants in the summer of 1942, resistance groups prepared for an uprising. In January 1943, the Nazis attempted to deport the remaining Jews, but they encountered armed resistance and suspended deportations. When the Nazis entered the ghetto to deport the remaining inhabitants in April 1943, about 750 organized ghetto fighters launched an insurrection. The resistance fighters were defeated on May 16, 1943. More than 56,000 Jews were captured and deported; about 7,000 were shot.

**Warsaw Uprising** An uprising by the non-Communist Polish resistance movement, the Polish Home Army (AK), to liberate Warsaw from German occupation and take control of the city before the Soviets arrived. The uprising started on August 1, 1944, as the Soviet army neared the city from the east. Facing a severe shortage of supplies and a calculated lack of support from the Soviets, the AK's approximately 40,000 troops were defeated by October 2, 1944. The revolt resulted in the deaths of over 150,000 civilians and the destruction of more than 25 per cent of Warsaw. The city was taken over by the Soviets and the pro-Soviet First Polish Army in January 1945, and a provisional government was installed.

**Wiesel, Elie** (1928–2016) A Romanian-born Jewish writer, professor and Holocaust survivor who was a human rights activist. Among numerous other prizes, Wiesel was awarded the Nobel Peace Prize in 1986. His most well-known book, *Night*, recounts his experience in Auschwitz and Buchenwald and is widely considered one of the most important works of Holocaust literature.

**WIZO (Women's International Zionist Organization)** An organization founded in England in 1920 to help women and children in what was then British Mandate Palestine and is now Israel. WIZO is currently the largest women's Zionist organization in the world.

**Yad Vashem** Israel's official Holocaust memorial centre and the world's largest collection of information on the Holocaust, established in 1953. Yad Vashem, the World Holocaust Remembrance Center, is dedicated to commemoration, research, documentation and education about the Holocaust. The Yad Vashem complex in Jerusalem includes museums, sculptures, exhibitions, research centres and the Garden of the Righteous Among the Nations.

**Yiddish** A language derived from Middle High German with elements of Hebrew, Aramaic, Romance and Slavic languages, and written in Hebrew characters. Spoken by Jews in east-central Europe for roughly a thousand years, it was the most common language among European Jews before the Holocaust. There are similarities between Yiddish and contemporary German.

**Yom Kippur** (Hebrew; day of atonement) A solemn day of fasting and repentance that comes eight days after Rosh Hashanah, the Jewish New Year, and marks the end of the High Holidays. *See also* Rosh Hashanah.

**Zionism** A movement promoted by the Viennese Jewish journalist Theodor Herzl, who argued in his 1896 book *Der Judenstaat (The Jewish State)* that the best way to resolve the problem of antisemitism and persecution of Jews in Europe was to create an independent Jewish state in the historic Jewish homeland of biblical Israel. Zionists also promoted the revival of Hebrew as a Jewish national language.

**Zündel, Ernst** (1939–2017) A German-born writer and publisher of materials promoting anti-Jewish sentiments and Holocaust denial. From 1958 to 2000, Zündel lived in Canada and distributed neo-Nazi propaganda. In 1985 and 1988, he was convicted of reporting false news but was acquitted by the Supreme Court of Canada in 1992. Zündel was arrested in the United States in 2003 and then deported to Germany, where he was imprisoned for five years for incitement of racial hatred.

Photographs

1  Anita's father, Fisko (Fischel) (back row, second from the left), with his scouts group. Stryj, Poland, 1920s.

2  Anita's mother, Edzia (Ettel). Sambor, Poland, 1920s.

3  Anita's maternal grandfather, Hershel Gottlieb, and Anita's aunt Sala (Sally). Sambor, Poland, 1930s.

1　From left to right: Anita's mother, Edzia; her grandmother Gela; and her aunt
　　Sala. Sambor, Poland, 1930s.
2　Anita with her parents, Edzia and Fisko. Synowódzko Wyżne, Poland, 1937.

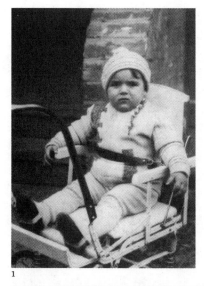

1 Anita. Synowódzko Wyżne, Poland, circa 1936.

2 Left to right (in back): Anita's father, Fisko; her aunt Yetta Zeisel; her mother, Edzia; her cousin (unknown name); her aunt Sala Stern; and Sala's husband, Victor Stern. (In front): Anita (right) with her cousins Romus and Zunia Stern. Krakow, 1938.

3 The forged birth certificate that Josef Matusiewicz commissioned to identify Anita as a Polish Catholic girl, Anna Jaworska.

1   Anita and Father Michal's housekeeper, Karola, in the small parish of Liczkowce,
    where Anita was hiding. Poland, circa 1943.

2   Anita and Karola. Liczkowce, circa 1943.

3   Anita doing her daily chore of feeding the chickens. Liczkowce, 1943–1944.

4   Anita with a friend of Father Michal's and his daughter. Anita is wearing the same
    shoes she had at the beginning of the war. Liczkowce, 1943–1944.

1 Anita (front, centre) with Father Michal (centre, with glasses) and members of the Liczkowce parish. Liczkowce, 1943–1944.

2 Anita with Josef's adopted daughter Lusia. Kluczbork, Poland, 1946.

3 Anita (front, centre) with the Matusiewicz family. From left to right: Paulina; Lusia (standing); and Josef, who is holding his great-niece Ola, Anita and his great-niece Basia. Poland, 1946.

1 Anita with her cousin Stefan's dog, Rex. Lodz, 1946.
2 Anita. Paris, 1947.
3 Anita. Paris, March 1948.

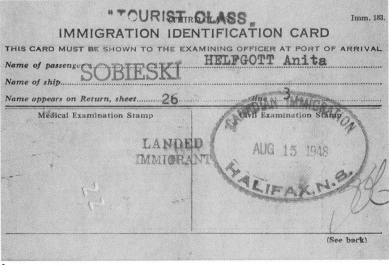

1   Anita, standing, with her aunt Sala and an unknown passenger on the SS *Sobieski* on the way to Canada. August 1948.

2   Anita's immigration card identifying her as a landed immigrant on her arrival in Canada.

Anita and her aunt Sala on their first day in Toronto. 1948.

1   Anita's family from New York with the Zeilers, who hosted Anita and her aunt
    Sala when they arrived in Canada: Left to right (standing): Anita's aunt Esther
    Begleiter; Anita's aunt Sala; and Anita's cousin Sylvia Korotkin. In front: Jean
    Zeiler with her children, Johnny and Cheryl.

2   Anita and her husband-to-be, Frank, at a dance. Toronto, 1952.

3   Anita and Frank on their wedding day. Toronto, June 5, 1955.

1 Anita with her family on the day of her wedding. From left to right (in back):
   Anita's brother-in-law, Paul Ekstein; Anita's in-laws, Ernest and Anna; Anita;
   Anita's husband, Frank; Anita's aunt Sala; and Anita's uncle Jack Goldstein. In
   front: Anita's sister, Terry. Toronto, June 1955.

2 Anita at her graduation from York University. Toronto, June 1985.

3 Article in the *Toronto Star* about Anita graduating from York University at the
   same time as her son Peter.

1

2

1   Anita at her childhood home in Synowódzko Wyżne. Ukraine, 1989.
2   The barn behind her childhood home in Synowódzko Wyżne, where Anita and
     her parents hid during the pogrom in 1941. Ukraine, 1989.

1

2

3

1 Anita in the Radłowice forest, where thousands of Jews from Sambor were murdered in 1942–1943. Poland, 1989.

2 Anita's sister, Terry Goldstein Root. Circa 1990s.

3 Anita's 60th birthday celebration. From left to right (back): Lydia White, Sheila Guttmann and Ethel Landis. In middle: Anita; her sister, Terry; and Molly Epstein. In front: Vera Price (sitting), Helen Greenspan and Golda Stern. Toronto, July 18, 1994.

1 At the ceremony honouring the Matusiewicz family as Righteous Among the Nations in the Israeli embassy in Poland. From left to right: Anita's daughter-in- law Lillian; Anita's grandchildren Stephanie and Michelle; Anita; the Israeli ambassador, Yigal Antebi, and his wife; Lusia; Anita's son Rick; and Anita's husband, Frank. Warsaw, Poland, 1998.

2 Anita listening to the bugler at Saint Mary's Church in Krakow, where her mother used to bring her when she was a child. Poland, 1998.

1 Anita and her husband, Frank, dancing at their grandson Cobi Lechem's bar mitzvah. Toronto, October, 2002.

2 Anita with her granddaughter Stephanie at her wedding to Michael Shapiro. From left to right: Anita's daughter-in-law Lillian; her son Rick; Anita; Stephanie; Michael; and Anita's granddaughter Michelle. Toronto, 2009.

1 Anita with her grandchildren attending a ceremony where she was honoured by the United Jewish Appeal (UJA). From left to right (in back): Cobi Lechem, Lara Lechem, Eli Ekstein, Leor Ekstein, Mike Shapiro, Stephanie Ekstein, Michelle Ekstein. In front: Anita with Orli Ekstein (left) and Yaelle Lechem (right). Toronto, 2010.

2 Anita with her niece-in-law Dori Ekstein at the Bełżec memorial while on March of the Living. Poland, 2011.

1  Anita with her children and grandchildren at her 80th birthday party. Back row: Ryan Sharpe, Alan Lechem, Lara Lechem, Jason Rose, Michelle Ekstein, Lillian Ekstein, Rick Ekstein, Stephanie Ekstein, Mike Shapiro, Leor Ekstein, Peter Ekstein. Front row: Yaelle Lechem, Ruth Ekstein, Anita, Stella Ekstein, Orli Ekstein. Toronto, July 2014.

2  Anita with her granddaughter Michelle (left) and Lusia's granddaughter Marta Kornacka. Poland, April 2017.

3  Anita's great-granddaughters, Emily (left) and Hallie (right) Shapiro. Toronto, 2019.

Anita. Toronto, 2017.

# Index

Abeles, Hannah (Frank's cousin), 84

Abeles, Ida (Frank's aunt), 84

Abeles, Karl, 83

Abeles, Leo (Frank's uncle), 84

Abeles, Mina (Frank's cousin), 84

Abella, Irving, 84

Abella, Rosalie, 128

Aix-les-Bains (France), 62

*Aktionen*, xviii–xx, 15, 19–20

Ala (Father Michal Kujata's niece), 53, 97, 112.

Ambrose, Thelma, 81

American army, 59

Anne Frank exhibit, 125

anti-Jewish legislation, xvii–xviii, 14–15, 19

*Arbeitslager* (forced labour camps), 51. *See also* Hochtief

Arc de Triomphe (Paris), 55

Auschwitz, xviii, 44, 61, 112

Auschwitz-Birkenau Memorial and Museum, 131

Australia, 43, 68

Babi Yar (Kiev), 113

Bandera, Stepan, xxiii

Banderowcy, 41–42

Banks, Barbara, 116

Basia (Father Michal Kujata's niece), 53, 97, 111–12.

Begleiter, Esther Silka (née Gottlieb, maternal aunt), 2, 7, 46, 67, 69, 71–72, 78–79, 94

Begleiter, Isidore (Iser, uncle), 7

Begleiter, Sarah (maternal great-grandmother), 115

Belgian Congo, 46, 57, 136

Bełżec (Poland), xviii, 20, 129–30, 132

Bergstein, Eve, 126–28

Beth David synagogue (Toronto), 105

Blair, Frederick Charles, 67

Bloch, Ernie (Frank's friend), 82–83, 85

B'nai Brith, 76–77, 81

Bogusz, Ania (cousin), 49, 51–52, 53, 57, 68, 138

Bogusz, Bogusia (cousin), 49–50, 68, 138; daughter Lotty, 138; son Leo, 138

Bogusz, Lucia (cousin), 49, 68, 138

Bogusz, Luis (cousin), 138

Bogusz, Stefan (formerly Horszowski, cousin), 49, 51–52, 53, 57, 68, 119, 138

Bogusz, Zygmunt (formerly Horszowski, cousin), 48, 49, 68, 138

Borochov Centre (Toronto), 93

British Mandate Palestine, 62, 65

Brünnlitz (Moravia), 47

bystanders, xvii, 141–42

Camp B'nai Brith, 76

Canada: immigration to, 67, 71, 83, 88

Canadian Coalition Against Terror (C-CAT), 136

Canadian Jewish Congress, 74

Canadian Jewish News, 127

Canadian National Exhibition (CNE, Toronto), 125

Canadian Society for Yad Vashem Award, 133

Cannes (France), 69

Caring for Aging Holocaust Survivors: A Practice Manual (David), 125

Carpathian Mountains (Poland), 48

Catholicism, xx–xxi, xxiii, 21, 25–26, 33, 36, 39, 45, 51, 56, 64, 105–6, 116–17

Catskills (New York), 78

Central High School of Commerce (Toronto), 77–78, 80

Central University of Venezuela, 68

chevra kadisha (burial society), 1

children, Jewish (during World War II), xix–xxii; hidden xx–xxiv, 37, 48, 62, 126–27

Circle of Care (Toronto), 107–8, 133

Claims Conference (The Conference on Jewish Material Claims Against Germany), 108

Cohen, Gerry (Frank's friend), 81

Colle, Mike, 133

Communion, 45, 117

Communism: in Poland, 106, 113, 119

Community Hebrew Academy of Toronto (CHAT), 132

Congregation Habonim (Toronto), 105

Conservative Party of Canada, 137

Cornwall, Ontario (Canada), 86

Czechoslovakia, Jews from, 82–84

Danek (Aunt Sala's former husband), 53, 57–58

David, Paula, 125

Demetriu, George, 70

Deutsche Emalwarenfabrik (Krakow), 47

Distrikt Galizien. See Galicia

Drohobycz (Poland), 3

École de jeunes filles (Paris), 58

Edelman, Hannah (friend in Paris), 59

Einsatzgruppen, xvii, 115

Ekstein, Anna ("Oma," Frank's
  mother), 84–88, 89–90, 137
Ekstein, Anita (née Helfgott): as
  Anna Jaworska, 31–50; birth
  of, 1, 3; birth of children, 101;
  102–3; Catholicism, 25–26, 28,
  36, 39, 45, 64, 105–6, 117; education, 58–59, 60, 73–74, 77–78,
  79–80, 108–9, 112; hidden in
  barn, xvi, 13; at Hochtief labour
  camp, 29–31; Holocaust education, 125–31, 133; immigration
  to Canada, 67–69, 71–72; in
  Israel, 135–36; Jewish identity,
  45, 105–6, 112, 117, 137, 141; in
  Katowice, 49–53; in Kluczbork,
  43–45, 48; in Liczkowce, 32–39;
  in Lodz, 52–53; in post-war
  Paris, 55–69; 112–13; pre-war
  childhood, 1–3, 5, 10–12; relationship with Frank, 81–84,
  90, 93–95; in Rozdół, 23–28; at
  sanatorium in Zakopane, 4–5;
  in Skole ghetto, xxi, 15, 16–23,
  28–29; trips to Eastern Europe,
  62, 111–12, 113–16, 117–18; volunteer work, 107–8, 124–26, 133;
  wedding, 93–94
Ekstein, Dori (niece), 130
Ekstein, Eli (grandson), 136
Ekstein, Ernest (Frank's father),
  84–88, 89–90, 105, 118, 137
Ekstein, Frank (husband), 81,
  84–88, 93, 105, 109, 125; death of,
  139–40; relationship with Anita,
  90, 34–95, 111; upbringing, 118

Ekstein, Leor (grandson), 132, 136
Ekstein, Lillian (née Wlosko,
  daughter-in-law), 117–18
Ekstein, Michelle (granddaughter),
  117–18, 120, 137, 141
Ekstein, Orli (granddaughter), 116,
  136
Ekstein, Paul (Frank's brother), 81,
  84–88, 93, 102
Ekstein, Peter (son), 102–3, 108–9,
  116; birth of, 124, 130, 136; ac-
  cident, 140
Ekstein, Richard Fred (Ricky, son),
  101, 104, 117–18, 124, 136–37, 140
Ekstein, Ruth Elaine (daughter),
  101, 104, 110, 112–13, 124, 130,
  136
Ekstein, Stella (née Amar, daugh-
  ter-in-law), 136
Eliach, Yaffa, 125
Elie Wiesel Holocaust Memorial
  Remembrance Medal, 133
Falcon Lumber (Toronto), 83, 86
Fantl, Eva (Frank's friend), 82, 85
Father Michal. See Kujata, Father
  Michal
Feldstein, Marian (friend), 55–56
Feldstein, Yetta (friend), 55–56
Frank and Anita Ekstein Holocaust
  Resource Collection (Toronto),
  126
Fritzie (Frank's friend), 82
Fry, Hedy, 133
Galicia (Poland), 14
Garden of the Righteous (Yad
  Vashem), 122

Gare du Nord (Paris) 57

Generalgouvernement, xvii, 14

German army, xv–xvii, 9, 15, 32, 32, 54; invasion of Poland, 61; invasion of Soviet Union, 12; occupation of Ukraine, 115. *See also* Gestapo; SS

Germans, ethnic, xvii

Gestapo, 27

Getzler, Herta (Aunt Sally's friend), 88

ghettos, xvii, xviii–xi, xix, xxi–xxii; police, xvii; *See also* Skole

Gibraltar, 70

Godula lumber mill (Sambor), 3

Golda (friend), 77

Goldstein, Jack (Aunt Sally's second husband), 60–62, 67–68, 75, 86–87, 94, 112, 137–38; arrival in Toronto, 75–76; death of, 103; return to Toronto, 102

Goldstein, Sala (Sally, née Gottlieb, aunt): general character of, 85, 87–88, 94, 103–104, 137–38; immigration to Canada, 67, 69–72, 73, 85–86; in Katowice, 46–48, 49–53; marriage to Danek, 53, 57–58; marriage to Jack Goldstein, 60–62, 67, 75; in Paris, 55–57, 58; pre-war relationship with, 2, 3, 5, 6, 10

Göth, Amon, 47

Gottlieb, Dorothy (aunt), 7, 78, 94

Gottlieb, Dwore (aunt), 2

Gottlieb, Elias (Eli, uncle), 2, 7, 67, 78, 94

Gottlieb, Gela (née Holtzman, maternal grandmother), 2, 8, 11

Gottlieb, Hershel (maternal grandfather), 2, 8, 11, 115

Gottlieb, Lea (aunt), 2

Gottlieb, Mordko Ber (uncle), 2

Gottlieb, Shelley (cousin), 7

Gottlieb, Stanley (cousin), 7

Gottlieb, Sureh Sara (aunt), 2

Gottlieb, Yetta (aunt), 2

Gould, Harry (Frank's friend), 82, 85

Government of Ontario (Canada), 133

Gray, Herb (Deputy Prime Minister, Canada), 133

Gypsies. *See* Roma

Halifax, Nova Scotia (Canada), 71

Hashomer Hatzair, 56

Hatikvah, 65

Helen (friend), 77, 79

Helfgott, Edzia (Ettel Rivka, née Gottlieb, mother), 1–2, 3, 6, 10, 45, 52, 125; disappearance, 19–20; during *Aktion*, 16, 19–20; hidden in barn, xvi, 13; marriage, 3, 8; monument inscription, 130; in pre-war period, 1–8

Helfgott, Elsa (aunt), 45, 57, 136

Helfgott, Fischel, (Fisko, father), xix, 1, 10, 27, 29–31, 36, 39, 42, 125; death of, 44, 96, 98–100, 118; final encounter with Anita, 31, 37; in hiding, xvi, 13; letter from, 45–46, 110; marriage, 3, 8; pre-war, 1–8, 124; saving Anita, 21–22

Helfgott, Irene (cousin), 57

Helfgott, Izio (paternal uncle), 2

Helfgott, Jenta (paternal grandmother), 1–2, 42, 116, 124

Helfgott, Moishe (Mojzesz
Mordko, paternal grandfather),
1–2, 8, 42, 116, 124

Helfgott, Saul (paternal uncle), 2,
45–46, 53, 57, 94

Helfgott, Toncha (née Bretler, paternal step-grandmother), 2, 42

hidden children, xx–xxiv, 37, 45,
48, 62, 126–27

Hidden Children Conference (New
York 1991), 127

Hochtief construction company
(Poland), 29

Hochtief labour camp (Poland), 28,
31, 44, 99, 100, 118

Holobutiv (Stryj, Poland), 116

Holocaust Centre of Toronto. See
Sarah and Chaim Neuberger
Holocaust Education Centre

Holocaust education, 122, 124–31,
133, 137, 141

Holocaust Memoirs: Jews in the
Lwow Ghetto, the Janowski
Concentration Camp,
and Deportees in Siberia
(Schoenfeld), 123

Holocaust Resource Program
(Toronto), 125

Holocaust survivors, 55, 61, 74–75,
87, 119, 124–27, 142

Horowitz, Artek (father's friend),
99, 100

Horowitz, Ania (née Bogusz), 138

Horowitz, Ryszard, 138

Horszowski, Gittel (née Gottlieb,
aunt), 2, 48

Horszowski family. See under
Bogusz

Hotel Wagram (Paris), 55

Humewood Public School
(Toronto), 73–74, 127

Husiatyn (Poland), 32

immigration, post-war. See under
specific country

Immigration Act of 1924 (United
States), 55

International Conference of
Jewish Child Survivors of
the Holocaust and Second
Generation (Toronto 2002), 128

Israel, 68, 135–136; Embassy of,
119–20

Israel Bonds Golda Meir
Leadership Award, 133

Jacobi, Shoshana, 125

Janowska concentration camp
(Lwów), 114

Jaworska, Anna (Anita's false identity), 31, 45

Jewish Camp Fund (Toronto), 76

Jewish education, 85; in Poland, 1,
3, 7; in Toronto, 105

Jewish identity, 51, 52, 62, 76, 106,
137,

JIAS (Jewish Immigrant Aid
Society), 73, 74

Kaddish, 113, 115, 118

Kamionkowie, Paulina, 13, 46, 114

Kamionkowie, Vasil (landlord in Synowódzko Wyżne), 4, 13, 24, 46, 114

Kanada barracks (Auschwitz), 61

Katowice (Poland), 46, 48, 49–53

Kennedy, President John F., 135

Kibbutz Afek (Israel), 135

Kibbutz Yagur (Israel), 136

Kiev (Ukraine), 113

*kittel*, 8, 11

Kluczbork (Silesia), 44, 48, 53, 111

Kornacka, Marta (Lusia's grand-daughter), 117, 120–22

Kornacka, Marysia (née Młot, Lusia's daughter), 116–17, 120–22

Korotkin, Michael, 71–72, 140

Korotkin, Sylvia (née Begleiter, cousin), 71, 94

Korotkin, Ted, 71–72, 94

Krakow (Poland), 5, 6, 10, 46, 47, 48, 51, 61, 62, 112, 116

Krell, Dr. Robert, 128

Kristallnacht, xvii

Kujata, Father Michal, 32–34, 37–38, 53, 96, 97, 119

Kupferberg, Chana (paternal great aunt), 43

Kupferberg, Jetusia (cousin), 43

Kupferberg, Shanka (cousin), 43

labour camps, 29–31, 51. *See also* Hochtief labour camp

Landis, Ethel (friend), 104, 135

Landis, Harold (friend), 135

*Lebensraum*, xvi–xvii

Lechem, Alan (son-in-law), 136

Lechem, Cobi (grandson), 136

Lechem, Lara (granddaughter), 136

Lechem, Yaelle (granddaughter), 124, 136

Leipciger, Nate, 133

Leningrad (Siege of), 37

*Les Misérables*, 60

Liczkowce (Poland), 32–38, 96

*Little Women* (Alcott), 75

Lodz (Poland), 52–53

Łopuchowo forest (Tykocin, Poland), 130

Lviv. *See* Lwów

Lwów, 1, 3, 5, 38, 46, 52, 113–14

Lychkivtsi (Ukraine). *See* Liczkowce (Poland)

Majdanek, 44

March of the Living, 82, 116, 120, 122, 129–33, 141

Marie and Jack Freedman Memorial Award, 133

Marlene (friend), 77, 82

Matusiewicz, Josef, 21–28, 30, 36, 46, 48, 119, 121; correspondence with, 106; death of, 101, 106, 111; honoured as rescuer, 119–20; letters from, 90–91, 96–100; rescue of Anita, 31–32; return from Siberia, 44

Matusiewicz, Lusia. *See* Młot, Lusia

Matusiewicz, Paulina: character of 22, 24, 43–45; death of, 106, 111; honoured as rescuer, 119–20; relationship with Anita, 25, 26, 28, 38–39, 42, 50

McMaster University (Hamilton),

136

Metz family, 88

Michal, Father. *See* Kujata, Father Michal

Młot, Lusia (Emilia, née Matusiewicz), 22–24, 26, 36, 116–17, 119; correspondence with, 33, 90, 106; death of, 120; honoured as rescuer, 119–21; in Kluczbork, 43–45; in Rozdół, 38, 41; leaving Rozdół, 42; reunion with, 111–12

Molotov-Ribbentrop Pact, xv, 9, 12

Montreal (Canada), 71

Mont-Saint-Père (France), 59

Mount Hope (Hamilton), 84

Munich, 54

National Council of Jewish Women, 108

Nazi occupation: of Poland, xv–xvii, xx, 14–15. *See also* German army

Neuberger Holocaust Education Centre. *See* Sarah and Chaim Neuberger Holocaust Education Centre

Newton, Elaine, 108

New York, 7, 46, 55, 59, 68, 70, 78–79, 94

*None is Too Many* (Abella and Troper), 84

Novak, Helen (Tamara's false identity), 62, 63

OneFamily Fund, 136

Ontario Institute for Studies in Education (OISE, Toronto), 125

Operation Barbarossa, 12

Organization of Ukrainian Nationalists. *See* Banderowcy

Palace of Versailles (Paris), 59

Pani Karola (housekeeper in Liczkowce), 32, 34–38

Paradise Dress & Waist (Toronto), 73

Paris, 53, 55–58; Jewish community in, 59; refugees in, 57–59

Park Plaza Hotel (Toronto), 72

Passover, 11–12, 76, 105

Pearl (cousin), 7, 78–79, 94

Phil (cousin), 94

*Pianist, The*, 94

Pier 21 (Halifax), 71

Plaszow concentration camp, 47

pogrom, 13–14

Poland: Catholicism in, xix; ethnic Germans in, 43; *Generalgouvernement* in, xvii; German occupation of, xv–xvii, xx, 9, 10, 14, 61; Jewish education in, xvii, 1–3; liberation of, xxii; Soviet occupation of, xv–xvii, xxii, xxiii, 9–11, 37–38; Ukrainians in, xv–xvi

Polish army, 9, 47

Pope John Paul II, 36

Popper, Alois (Frank's uncle), 84

Popper, Doris, 85, 135

Popper, Heda (Frank's aunt), 84

Popper, Julek (Joe, cousin), 42, 82, 84

Popper, Miriam (Macia, née Helfgott, paternal aunt), 2, 42,

46, 116

Popper, Richard (cousin), 82, 84, 135

Prague, 54, 118

Przemyśl (Poland), 51, 52

Radłowice forest (Poland), 115–116, 117

Rae, Bob (Premier of Ontario), 133

Red Army. *See* Soviet army

refugees, 55, 65, 67, 74, 83

Regensburg (Germany), 54

Renee (cousin), 7, 78–79, 94

rescuers, xvi, xx, xxiii, 21–22, 31, 48, 53, 62, 90, 119–20, 142

Righteous Among the Nations, 119–20, 122

Ringelblum, Emanuel, xxi–xxii

Roma, 11–12

*Roman de Renart, Le*, 60

Root, Michael (Terry's husband), 107

Root, Tamara (Terry, née Goldstein), 61–64, 67–68, 79, 86–89, 94, 106–7; arrival in Toronto, 75–76; in Paris, 112; return to Toronto, 102

Rosh Hashanah, 8, 76

Rubenstein, Eli, 130, 131

Rusia (landlady in Toronto), 82

Ruzia (aunt and uncle's tenant), 93

Rozdil (Ukraine). *See* Rozdół (Poland)

Rozdół (Poland), 23–28; evacuation of, 42; Jews in, 27–28, 38–39, 41, 44

Sambor (Ukraine), 2, 3, 8, 11–12, 59, 67, 81, 115, 117; ghetto, 115

Sarah and Chaim Neuberger Holocaust Education Centre, 124–25, 126, 128–29, 136, 141

Schindler, Oskar, 47, 54–55, 88, 138

*Schindler's List*, 54

Schoenfeld, Chaim (Joachim, great-uncle), 114, 123–24, 137

Schoenfeld, Ola (great-aunt), 124

Schoenfeld, Tatiana (married to Uncle Chaim), 124, 137

Schreiben (father's friend), 99, 100

Schwammberger, Josef (SS Sergeant), 51–52

Segal (family next door), 3; Freddie, 3, 15

Seldon, Henry (Frank's friend), 86

Seldon, Mary, 86

Senior Care. *See* Circle of Care

Shabbat, 7, 76

Shafrir, Josef, 135–136

Shafrir, Rachel (Rela, née Helfgott, paternal aunt), 2, 6, 42, 43, 124, 135–36

Shapiro, Emily Joelle (great-grand-daughter), 141

Shapiro, Hallie (great-granddaughter), 141

Shapiro, Michael (grandson-in-law), 141

Shapiro, Stephanie (née Ekstein, granddaughter), 117–18, 120, 137, 141

Shaw Business College (Toronto), 83

Sheila (friend), 77, 94

*Shtetl Memoirs: Jewish Life in*

*Galicia under the Austro-Hungarian Empire and the Reborn Poland, 1898–1939* (Schoenfeld), 123
Siberia, 44
Signoret, Simone, 139
Silesia, xxiii, 43. *See also* Kluczbork
Silverman, Loretta, 72, 75
Silverman, Sia, 72, 75
Skole (Poland), 16, 98–99; ghetto, xviii–xi, 16–22; liquidation of, 28–29, 46
Slonim, Rabbi Reuben, 93
Snyder, Timothy, xv
Solange (friend), 59–60, 112
Soviet army, xvi, xxii, 12, 37, 38–39, 41
Soviet Union: German invasion of, 12; occupation of Poland, xv–xvii, xxii, xxiii, 9–11, 37–38
Spellman, Leo, 94
SS (Schutzstaffel), xvii, 29, 47, 51. *See also* German army
SS *Sobieski*, 69–71
Stahelberger (SS officer), 29
Stalin, Joseph, xv
Star of David, 56
Stern, Romus (cousin), 6, 47
Stern, Victor (uncle), 6, 47, 71
Stern, Zunia (cousin), 6, 47
Strupp, Rachel. *See* Shafrir, Rachel
Stryj (Poland), 1, 8, 10, 42–43, 46, 116, 117; Jews in, 43; river, 17
Switzerland, 56
Synowódzko Wyżne (Poland), 1, 12, 17, 29, 42, 96, 98, 113, 114, 117–18;

pogrom in, 13–14
Szpilman, Władysław, 94
Szusz, Mr. (Frank's boss), 102
Talmud Torah (Sambor), 2
Tarnopol (Poland), 38
Tatra Mountains (Poland), 4
Tip Top Tailors (Toronto), 75, 80
Tops Restaurant (Toronto), 82
*Toronto Star*, 109
Treblinka, xviii, 44
Troper, Harold, 84
Tykocin (Poland), 130–31
UJA. *See* United Jewish Appeal
Ukraine, 1, 113; German occupation of, 115
Ukrainians, 113, 115; in Poland, xv–xvi, xxiii, 13; policemen, 27, 41, 100
Ukrainian Insurgent Army, 41–42
Union Station (Toronto), 71
United Jewish Appeal (UJA), 116, 125, 128, 136
United Nations, 65
United States: immigration to, 7, 67; Immigration Act of 1924, 55, 67
University of Illinois at Urbana-Champaign, 107
University of Minnesota, 107
University of Toronto, 107, 125
University of Warsaw, 68
Vaughan Road Collegiate (Toronto), 74
Ve'ahavta Tikun Olam Humanitarian Award, 133
Venezuela, 68, 138

Vera (friend), 77
Vis, Leonard, 128
Warsaw, 53–54, 68, 119–120; ghetto,
    xxi
Warsaw Ghetto Uprising, 53, 116
Weiser (landlord, Toronto), 75
Weston Forest Group, 136–37
*We Were Children Just Like You*, 125
Wiesel, Elie, 122
*Wizard of Oz, The*, 59
WIZO (Women's International
    Zionist Organization), 2
World War II, xv–xvi; outbreak, 9
Yad Vashem (Jerusalem), 118,
    119–20, 122, 141
Yiddish language, 6–7
Yom Kippur, 8, 76
York University (Toronto), 108–9,
    136
Zakopane (Poland), sanatorium,
    4–5, 48
Zeiler, Cheryl, 72, 75, 93
Zeiler, Jean, 93
Zeiler, Johnny, 72, 75
Zeiler, Sidney, 67, 72–73, 75
Żegota (Polish Council to Aid
    Jews), xx. *See also* rescuers
*Zette: histoire d'une petite fille*
    (Margueritte), 59
Zionism, 1, 2, 56
Zündel, Ernst, 123

The Azrieli Foundation was established in 1989 to realize and extend the philanthropic vision of David J. Azrieli, C.M., C.Q., M.Arch. The Foundation's mission is to support a wide spectrum of initiatives in education and research. The Azrieli Foundation is an active supporter of programs in the fields of education, the education of architects, scientific and medical research, and the arts. The Azrieli Foundation's many initiatives include: the Holocaust Survivor Memoirs Program, which collects, preserves, publishes and distributes the written memoirs of survivors in Canada; the Azrieli Institute for Educational Empowerment, an innovative program successfully working to keep at-risk youth in school; the Azrieli Fellows Program, which promotes academic excellence and leadership on the graduate level at Israeli universities; the Azrieli Music Project, which celebrates and fosters the creation of high-quality new Jewish orchestral music; and the Azrieli Neuro-developmental Research Program, which supports advanced research on neurodevelopmental disorders, particularly Fragile X and Autism Spectrum Disorders.